TALLAWUDJAH CREEK

... and Me

Elizabeth Webb OAM

TALLAWUDJAH CREEK

... and Me

by

Elizabeth Webb OAM

Tallawudjah Creek ... and Me
by Elizabeth Webb OAM

Text, photos and all illustrations - Copyright © Elizabeth Webb 2024
All rights reserved.

This book or parts thereof may not be reproduced in any form, stored in a retrieval system, or transmitted in any form by any means - electronic, mechanical, photocopy, recording or otherwise - without prior written permission of the publisher.

Published by Nenge Books, Australia, February 2024
ABN 26809396184
Email: nengebooks1@gmail.com
www.nengebooks.com

Design and desktop by Nenge Books.

Cover photo - Holder children in their first creek crossing near their new house, 1928. From left: Bessie, 'Mac', Daphne, Agnes & Charlie.
Drawings on cover, pages 2 and 9, and chapter header by Les Webb.

ISBN 978-0-6459597-1-0

Dedication

I would like to dedicate this book to my parents, Sarah Jane Etta and Thomas Graham Holder, who built their home in the upper reaches of the Tallawudjah Creek. They created a loving home and an enriching environment for our family. It also included our neighbours and the road and timber workers camped close by. It is this immediate area of Tallawudjah that is covered in this book.

Contents

Dedication	v
Foreword	ix
1. The Lure of Gold	1
2. The Creek - Tallawudjah and Tallongal	6
3. The Simpsons featuring Granny and Grandad	10
4. Mum and Dad	22
5. Us Kids	38
6. Our New Home	46
7. Aunty Milda and Uncle Jack	58
8. My First School	63
9. Connecting with the Outside	77
10. Our Neighbours	79
11. Influence of the Railway	82
12. Characters of the Bush	86
13. Reflections	94

Foreword

This book is not something I had been planning on writing. It happened because of my 100th birthday celebrations and the many conversations and reflections that happened in the lead up to my big day on 29th May 2022, and since encouraged by my son Peter. In my quiet time, my thoughts now are very much centred on the creek of my childhood—my beginnings, the creek of my youth. A further thought reminded me that it was also the creek of my mother's youth. She was born there on the 5th November 1895.

I was attending two different functions in the Glenreagh community during 2022 and found myself conversing on both occasions with residents who had spent some years living at Tallawudjah Creek. One lady has spent the last 13 years living there, and the other had lived there for some 8 years before shifting away. During our conversations I remarked that I had gone to school there. They were wide eyed with surprise and somewhat disbelieving.

Question after question came quick and fast. Where was the school? Where did you live? How many kids went to the school? Was it a Government School? How did the people at that time earn their living? Plus, lots more questions were asked.

The history of Tallawudjah Creek needs to be told as it is not only my history - its history is shared with the close-by Glenreagh community. In many ways this story is part of the history of the growing Glenreagh community that straddles the Orara River.

Here is a little history on just where my childhood playground is situated on the beautiful North Coast of New South Wales.

Tallawudjah Creek commences flowing down from what is known as The Valley near Dorrigo where the winter cold winds originate. The Creek joins the Orara River at Glenreagh, a Timber Town located almost midway on the back road between Grafton and Coffs Harbour. The Orara River then flows into the mighty Clarence River, upstream of Grafton, before the pristine Tallawudjah waters find the ocean at Yamba.

And Me. I am Elizabeth Webb OAM (nee Holder), a granddaughter of Charles and Elizabeth Simpson who settled at Tallawudjah Creek in 1886-87. This is the story of my beginnings, the first sixteen years when I lived at Tallawudjah. They are my memories. Where possible I have attempted to check the accuracy of what is written. However, there are not many around today from my early years for me to check with.

Elizabeth (Bessie) Webb

Glenreagh, NSW, October 2023

1. The Lure of Gold

I 'arrived' at the Creek because of my Grandad, Charles Simpson, one of the first white settlers to arrive there in 1886-87. For the first fifteen years after his arrival Grandpa was known as a miner.

Gold had been discovered at nearby Nana Glen in the early 1880s, and news of the lucrative finds appear to have spread quickly as people came from afar to seek the elusive metal. It was a short distance from what was known as the Nana Glen Goldfields to the head of Tallawudjah Creek (on early maps it is called Tallongal at its headwaters). It was always called Tallawudjah by my ancestors.

John Nicholson is credited with taking up the first lease at Tallawudjah Creek in 1882. The successful miners who worked on the Nana Glen goldfields ventured further afield and are credited with setting up the first crushing battery at Tallawudjah. This was known as the Old Battery where the old China Pear trees grew.

The early miners went back and forth for supplies and other needs via McPhersons Road. It branches off to the west from

Orara Way at the top of the rise past Coldwater Creek. Some may have taken the Ellems Quarry Road which branches off Orara Way just before the Coldwater Creek causeway crossing. The bush tracks that abounded in those days came over the hills and down the decline to come out on land quite close to the goldfields and the old Tallawudjah Battery.

It was in this lonely, heavily timbered and isolated place with no facilities that Charles Simpson and his family settled. On all his legal documents he called himself a miner but diligent research at the Mining Records Office did not locate any lease in his name.

Other research found these leases cost one Pound ($2) per year and the names on these leases were changing annually as the gold returns dwindled for the working miners. Some of the names of these gold leases were The Joker, Homeward Bound, Caledonian, Red White and Blue, Miner's Bride, Day Dawn and Clondyke.

By the turn of the century gold was very hard to find. Recent research indicates a few reasons as the veins varied in thickness from a few inches to three or four feet. Shoots were short and narrow and lenticular veins did not exist to deep depths. However, the total amount of gold won from this area exceeded 30,000 ounces.

Many miners left to seek their fortunes elsewhere. Meantime, some who came looking for gold and had agricultural backgrounds, bought land and stayed as they saw the potential of their surroundings. Their families had grown and they were seeking settled lifestyles of their own. My Grandad, Charles, had ceased working for the miners as the gold rush up the creek hadn't flourished as expected.

Roads and railways were spreading out all over the country and the need for timber was gaining popularity. These early settlers never forgot about the 'lure' with the odd search over the years meeting with modest success. As late as 1942, an Uncle of mine paid for his groceries at the Glenreagh General Store with gold mined from the Creek.

A newspaper report dated May 1917 under the heading of Results of Gold, Copper, and Iron Ore Mining provides a unique insight.

W. Shipman raised and treated 13 tons of stone from his mine at Tallawudjah Creek for a yield of 25 ounces of gold valued at 90 pounds ($180). At the Bushman's Range Mine, Mole Creek, H. Jones raised and treated 12 tons of stone for 20 ounces of gold valued at 75 pounds ($150).

When the first Glenreagh History book (Glenreagh 1858-1983) was printed in 1983, research provided a docket from the family of Mr A. Pritchett that is reproduced on page 11 of that book. It is not dated but states the value of a parcel of gold being over $272 pound ($544).

Later a second Battery was erected a little south of the Avery's Creek Junction. It was on the creek side of the road before where the Simpsons Spur Road branches off to the west. This Battery was still operating intermittingly as late as the early 1930s. I remember a man named Dick McKay showing us kids how it worked and seeing the tiny flecks of gold being caught on the special areas as the crushed ore was carried by the water away from the Battery.

However, the interest is still alive and well as the search for gold goes on today– hope, they say, springs eternal in the human breast. The creek of my youth is still there and so is the Lure of the Gold.

Road sign in Glenreagh.

The poem following was written after a trip we made in 1990 to find the site of the old pub on the Nana Glen goldfields. It was from there that the miners went to the head of Tallawudjah Creek. Shortly after, I woke at 3 am one morning with these words going around in my head. I got up and wrote them down and then went back to sleep!

The Old Gold Town

Vines loop down from tall tree tops
Touching the stream here and there,
Whilst the soft distant call of the lyre bird
Stirs the peace of the morning air,
The old pub site is deserted
Yet somehow the voices are there,
Mingling together in mateship
Or clasping a hand in despair.

There are no men now on the diggings
On the site by the rippling creek,
Old shafts and a few broken relics speak
Of the gold they came to seek.
Grey rocks where cool water ripples
On its journey down through the glen
Keep natures secrets well hidden
From hard working mining men.

They toiled weary hours to prosper
They searched and followed the seam
Now the bustle and noise of those gold fever days
Have gone from the forest serene.
Though life moves onwards and values change
Man will seek and follow a dream
Beauty and treasure are still by the creek
In tall trees and soft shades of green.

Copyright © Elizabeth Webb 1990

2. The Creek - Tallawudjah and Tallongal

This creek with two names starts some 90 kilometres southwest of Grafton and west of Glenreagh in a narrow valley that eventually turns towards Dorrigo. Tallawudjah is believed to be an aboriginal word meaning ironbark. On some early maps the name Tallongal, was also given to the upper portion of this creek. The creek, now officially gazetted as Tallawudjah Creek, travels some winding distance in length. It was in the upper reaches of the surrounds of this creek that gold was discovered in the early 1880's

Miners searching for the elusive gold were the first white settlers to come to the area. As the population was growing on the settled parts of NSW, the word soon spread about fortunes to be made on the north coast of the state.

Simpson, Shipman, Gray, McPherson, Symonds and Garratt are some of the family names that settled on the upper reaches of the Creek. Hooson, Ellem, Darke, Green and Pritchett are families that settled on the creek closer to the village of

Glenreagh and their histories are recorded in my book titled 'Glenreagh, A Town of Promise'.

Many of these families had a friendship or were known to each other before they came here from the Illawarra and Robertson areas on the New South Wales south coast.

After their arrival by steamer at the wharf, that was located on the South Grafton side of the Clarence River, the families would have travelled along the winding dirt road, most likely by mail coach or bullock team, to their land. A likely stop on this journey would have been at the Glen Righ Homestead, built in 1858, on land now known as 41 James Street, Glenreagh. At that time James Street was the main street coming into Glenreagh after crossing Tallawudjah Creek. Their form of travel to their property, some 20 kilometres away up Tallawudjah Creek, can only be imagined.

Recorded history shows a Progress Association was formed at Tallawudjah Creek in 1891. Some four years later 200 pounds was allocated to form the Tallawudjah Creek Road. One can only assume that it was a bush track of a rather rugged nature at that time.

In 1980, I was living in Llandilo near Penrith NSW, and my bus driving duties were over, and our kids had all wed and left home. My husband, Les, was building a home for one of our kids and I was often home with my thoughts. I found myself thinking about Tallawudjah Creek, and a poem came into my head. It was the anniversary of my father's death, which occured on the 21 August 1949. I wrote the poem below on 21 August 1980.

I returned with Les to live near the Creek of my Youth at Glenreagh on 28 November 1982.

Tallawudjah Creek

It lazily wended its way past the school
Through the farms and over crossings it went,
At flood time it raged as it broke o'er the banks
Then returned when its fury was spent.

A long time ago the settlers came
They fossicked the fresh winding stream,
The women folk shared in the harsh bush life
Together they worked for their dream.

Their homes were built of rough bush slabs
With shingles to keep out the weather,
The white washed walls reflected the glow
As the fire shadows mingled together.

The creek was the playground for all who lived
On the cleared fertile pieces of land,
And the little lone grave like a sentinel stood
Spoke a grief they could all understand.

The cutters rode by on their horses each morn
To be in the bush at first light,
The women washed clothes down by the stream
And the children skipped stones with delight.

The bullockies travelled the long dusty road
Down the lane to the mill miles away
They called to the leaders as they strained on the yokes
And the wagons rolled slowly each day.

The creek is still lazily flowing along
But where is my playground of youth?
The one room school, like the settlers, has gone
And the road has a different route.

And the shadows that danced on the white washed walls
As I played by the firelight's glare,
Like the spirit and folk of that era have gone
But the creek of my youth is still there.

Copyright © Elizabeth Webb 1981

3. The Simpsons featuring Granny and Grandad

To get me into the Tallawudjah Creek story, I need to commence with my grandparents, Charles and Elizabeth Simpson. Elizabeth was born at Jamberoo on 28 January 1858, the eldest child of Thomas and Jane Keevers (nee Hunt). Nothing is known of her childhood other than she grew up on a farm at Druewalla and she was awarded book prizes for being a good Sunday School student.

We do know that my Granny was the granddaughter of Sgt. William Keevers who had fought at the Battle of Waterloo in 1812, and survived. He later came, in 1823, to Australia with the 3rd Regiment of Foot, in charge of convicts. He was awarded a Waterloo Medal for 1812, which is now in the War Memorial in Canberra. He is also credited with training the first Mounted Police in NSW. His photo is displayed in their museum in Redfern, Sydney.

Charles Simpson, a twin with brother Richard, was born on the 29 June 1855 at Dapto. His parents, Charles (Senior) and wife Hannah (Lambert), had arrived from Buckland, Berkshire (UK) on the Royal Saxon with one son, Giles, on the 19 July 1848. Both parents stated they could read and write and they were farmers.

Documents record Elizabeth and Charles's marriage at the Church of Resurrection at Jamberoo on 28 March 1878. Elizabeth was 20 years of age, and her father, Thomas, gave his permission.

Elizabeth & Charles Simpson 1920s

They went on to have four children and were reported at one stage to be living at Shellharbour, NSW. The Illawarra district, at this time, was well known as the 'food basket of the colony', and it was experiencing a severe drought. It is believed that the drought, plus overcrowding on family farms, mingled with the stories of prosperity on the north coast of NSW, caused many settlers to seek a new beginning.

Charles and Elizabeth, like many other residents living in the Illawarra district, would have been impressed with the knowledge filtering through about the rich north coast of NSW. Many words were read and spoken of the fortunes that were to be made. Gold had been discovered in several places, and the huge cedar trees that were growing in abundance in the rainforests were there for the cutting.

Grafton, situated on the Clarence River, had been discovered some fifty years prior to their arrival and the cedar cutters had begun arriving in the area. Some settlers had driven their sheep down the most hazardous route from the Tablelands to the 'Settlement' as Grafton was then named. Governor Fitzroy renamed it after his Grandfather - The Duke of Grafton.

As early as 1839 Captain A.S. Perry reported that a vessel of some 160 tons was being constructed on the banks of the river that is now known as South Grafton. Steamers regularly sailed along the coast of New South Wales and they also serviced the busy port of Kiama on the South Coast, which was easily reached from Jamberoo. These vessels not only carried all types of cargo, but also passengers on these trips up and down the coast.

It is on one of those vessels that the Simpsons came to Tallawudjah. It is believed in family history, that Charles came at the request of his brother William Simpson, in either late 1886 or the early months of 1887. My grandparents had four children when they arrived and their fifth child, a son, was born on his mother's birthday, 28 January 1888, when they were living at Tallawudjah Creek. Mary Shipman is named on his birth certificate as assisting at his birth.

It is also known Granddad had a building ready to house the family and that he settled further along the Creek than his brother William.

Some of my family members think that William Simpson was here before his brother Charles, while others think they came together. We do know that William's selection was closer

Simpson property, Eliza's trees far right, with bullocky crossing the creek (1922).

to Glenreagh and Charles's selection was at the most southern end of the Creek and closest to the goldfields. However, both properties adjoined one another and later Charles was able to purchase William's property.

Charles and Elizabeth settled on a fertile flat section of land bounded by Tallawudjah Creek on the eastern boundary. Their eldest child Eliza planted some fruit trees on this property which are still standing and are known by family members as 'Eliza's Trees'. Sadly, Eliza died in 1889 from a serious fall from a tree stump on the property and is buried in South Grafton Cemetery.

Eliza's trees

Near the end of the orange trees, buried on the property, there were the two small graves of William Simpson's two little children who died in 1892. A post and rail fence was built around these graves, and as kids we were inclined to climb and walk on the rails, but Mum was forever watchful and disallowed any playing in that area. There was a pink climbing rose growing all over the graves and the fence.

William struggled with the grief after the loss of his wife Jane and children, and soon after his loss he decided to ask his brother Charles to take over his property. Because of the sadness of his daughter Eliza dying at the top Simpson property, Grandad Charles decided to take up the offer to buy his brother William's property and move into William's home.

The first homes were known to be 'Rough and Ready', made from large sheets of bark, cut from the trees that were easily available, and quick to assemble. They were called Galleys and were used to make a quick kitchen until a more substantial building was built.

Simpson home at Glenreagh c.1914

A 1924 map of the area shows that a further property, south of what became known as the Junction, was in the name of Wolseth. Richard John Simpson, Charles's youngest son, purchased this property and had a home built there before his marriage in 1927. This property extended to the creek crossing south beyond the junction of what was then known as Avery's Junction.

Elizabeth, Sgt. William's granddaughter and my Grandma, clearly illustrated a strong organising character during her lifetime. This was certainly needed in those early days of settlement at Tallawudjah Creek and for that matter in the Glenreagh district as well. Elizabeth moved from Tallawudjah Creek when her husband Charles purchased the property about three kilometers south of Glenreagh on the southern roadway going from Glenreagh to Nana Glen. This move with their three single daughters took place about 1910/11 and this property was farmed from then until her death in June 1936. In their latter years this was with assistance from share farmers as Charles had passed away in 1931.

Lizzie & Sarah at Glenreagh, c.1916

There is a lasting memory of her energy and enthusiasm for Glenreagh with the Anglican Church Bell Tower that was erected in 1927. In a newspaper report at the time of the event it credited Elizabeth's organising ability in having the Church Bell erected free of debt.

It is known in the family that the three Simpson girls Annie, Sarah and Lizzie were all born on the Tallawudjah property. Annie the eldest girl was in 1893, Sarah 1895 (who became my mother), and Lizzie in 1898.

Simpson descendents under the fruit trees in 1987 - L to R: Noelene Schaffer, Lizzie, Bessie Webb & Rexie Simpson

In 1905 Grandad decided to add a new kitchen and improve the homestead on William's property. A letter had arrived advising that Elizabeth's father was very ill at Jamberoo, on the South Coast of NSW. The decision was made that while the new addition was being built, Grandad Charles and the male members of the family could care for themselves. Grandma Elizabeth could take the three girls down the coast by boat and see the girl's grandparents for the first time.

My mother and my aunts often recalled that boat trip in their later lives as all three girls were very sea-sick all the way down and on the way home. After a stay of some weeks, Elizabeth's father had recovered somewhat, but as Elizabeth was packing to come home in preparation to sail the next day, her mother passed away suddenly. Her father, Thomas, went on to live for another two years and passed in 1907.

When I first researched my Grandad Charles' history, I found he was recorded as a miner but I could not find a lease in his name. I did find that he was paid one pound a week (two dollars) for his horse and slide and himself to take the quartz out to the batteries for crushing. I also found that many of the leases changed names each year which led me to believe that the returns were not very robust.

While Charles worked on the gold leases, Elizabeth's eldest son Bill, who at that time was some 11 years of age, held the reins and drove the horse, while she held the plough in the ground as they toiled to develop the farm.

By the turn of the century the search for gold had diminished somewhat and most of the miners had moved on to richer fields. Grandad Charles became disillusioned with the gold prospects and he became busy developing his large property. He was also engaged in doing fencing jobs for others as more families settled and took up land.

The public road went through their property and there were slip-rails across the roadway adjacent the homestead. The roadway at that time turned east to cross the creek and travel a short distance before crossing it again. The road went on through Granddad Charles' top property and past Avery's waterhole on the left, where the road goes across Morning Star Creek before continuing to the goldfields.

My Grandma Elizabeth received an inheritance from her father's will after he died in 1907 and she was able to purchase considerable acres of land adjoining the homestead property. The Simpsons prospered and two of the sons, now young men, had a pit saw "one up - one down" type of Timber Mill. They were busily preparing the timber for their homes they were building on nearby Simpson land, in preparation for their approaching marriages.

Grandad Charles found himself working for other people at this time. He had been employed by Mr Sweeney from Glenreagh to work on a property some 3 kms south of Glenreagh on the Nana Glen Road. This property had two homes on it and Charles and Elizabeth moved with the three girls over into one of the homes. Their married son Albert, known as Bert, and his wife Martha managed the Tallawudjah Creek property.

The following snippet is taken from an old undated letter from my elderly Aunt Lizzie when I was recording our family history in 1988.

Dad was working for Mr Sweeney when Mr Sweeney's lease on the property was up and we thought we would have to shift back up the Creek but Mr Snodgrass who owned the property decided to sell and leave and Daddy decided to buy it. Bert and Martha were managing Granny's farm up the creek so that is when we settled there and started milking cows. It was a busy life Annie was getting married; the Church was being built in Glenreagh and World War 1 was on. Your mother married in 1918 and they took over Granny's farm up Tallawudjah and Bert and Martha came over here to help Daddy and me on this farm, they eventually bought their own place next door and shifted into their own home but still helped Daddy here after I married in 1921. Sadly, my brother Bert died in 1927 and there were share farmers here on this property until it was sold after Granny died.

I don't know why my grandparents decided to leave Tallawudjah Creek and buy the Glenreagh farm but I think it was the lack of a permanent school up the creek. There were many starts and stops at full time and half time schools. In later years, when researching family history, I found letters written by Granny to the Inspector at the time asking that there be a fulltime school at Tallawudjah Creek or she would be sending her children down to Glenreagh School.

She was a lady that needed to be close to the action. She had her three girls taught the piano by a lady from Nana Glen who came by sulky to the Tallawudjah home. At some time later, when the Simpson girls were older and lived at Glenreagh, they were taught by Mrs Alda Orr-Morris, a well known music teacher, who came from Grafton to give lessons at the hotel.

All the girls could do really lovely crochet work, with my Mum continuing with this until late in her life. They were taught this skill by the wife who was boarding at the hotel while her husband was working on the construction of the Glenreagh to Dorrigo railway.

After the railway was opened in 1924, a dentist come to the hotel from Dorrigo and I recall my brother, for some reason, had to visit him for some problem he had with his teeth as a child.

My Grandma Elizabeth was a hard worker and a great organiser while Grandad Charles was a gentle old man who just loved to sit on his front veranda and tell his grandkids stories about Mt Baldy and the many waterfalls that come and go during the wet season. He was not a well man at this stage and was not able to do any heavy work. He had a beautiful small front garden filled with lovely old, perfumed roses and he got great pleasure in telling his grandchildren the history of the plants.

He also had a wonderful way of teasing. The mail was delivered with the paper each day by the mailman into their letterbox down at the farm entrance. He would ask us kids to run down as quietly as we could and get the paper for him to read first. Granny liked to read the paper first, but usually with her being busy cooking inside, it was a game for him to tease her and also for us grandkids to enjoy being part of the challenge.

I was astounded when I came back to Glenreagh in 1982 to see a Bagawa Creek sign, just south of my grandparent's place. This is the Creek that went through my grandparent's property and my grandparents called it Barkaway Creek. My Dad and Mum used to laugh about the name that brought them together. I asked around recently and found that Mick Towells can recall it from his childhood as Barkaway Creek. When researching my family history in the 1980's I also saw it spelt on a very old map that my cousin had as Barkaway.

In April 2023 I saw a quiz question printed in a local paper wanting the reader to name a river in NSW. The name was *Baarka*, an Aboriginal word for bank.

The Simpson girls, by this time, were getting married and this meant that my grandparents needed help on the farm. Annie had wed in 1914, and now with second daughter Sarah leaving, the decision was made that their son Bert, who was working the Tallawudjah property, purchase the adjoining property to his parents at Glenreagh. Now known as the Howlett property, Bert, with his wife Martha, was able to help his parents on the farm.

I think one of the reasons had something to do with the school closing. I know my mother had finished her school years but her younger sister hadn't at that stage. I do know that Grandad was doing fencing jobs on various properties for people and he was engaged to do some fencing for a Mr Snodgrass that was on a property some four kilometres south of Glenreagh. By this time two of his sons were married and living on nearby family properties up the Creek. Harry Simpson had two children of school age, so he and his family moved to Repton to be near his wife's family and to get his kids educated. He had a car and would visit us from time to time.

Bert Simpson stayed on the home farm and my grandparents purchased the Glenreagh property and moved in about 1911. My Granny and Grandad Simpson, who both came from farming backgrounds, could no doubt see the potential in this property.

Granny, Elizabeth Simpson (nee Keevers), was the oldest child in her family of twelve brothers and sisters. Family research tells us that Richard Keevers, Granny's brother, came to this area with her or soon after. He stayed a while; owned a block next door north to the Tallawudjah Creek school and his signature was on a request for a Receiving Office for mail at Tallawudjah Creek in 1889.

Richard didn't settle here, so I can only think the block was later sold, as he lived out his life in Jamberoo.

I found it interesting that my Granny's father, Thomas Keevers, was also a signatory on the request for a postal receiving office at Tallawudjah Creek.

Granny had never mentioned that part of history to me, I rather think they were visiting his daughter and his sister after the accidental death of Eliza Simpson, Thomas's grandchild.

Car being rescued from flood waters.

Bullockies sometimes stopped for a photo in front of our house, this one with a 100ft 'big load'

4. Mum and Dad

Remembering my parents now, I can recall how well suited they were and how their personalities blended together in creating such a safe, loving environment for us kids. This would not have been an easy task in those Depression years when the lack of any ready cash was felt all over the country. Us kids were not aware of the Depression at the time as we were mostly living off the land from Mum and Dad's efforts. Mum was fifteen years younger than Dad when they married but any age difference didn't seem to bother anyone back then.

Dad, Thomas Graham Holder, born on 11 November 1880 at the Malara goldfields, was 6 feet tall and of a solid build. He had the reputation of being a good worker and a very strong man who had been reared in the bush. Dad's father was a miner on the Malara goldfields with the family later relocating to Lionsville and the Washpool area at the head of the Clarence River. Some of Dad's sisters were employed to undertake kitchen wash-up duties at Yugilbar Castle.

Dad hadn't attended any school and had been taught to read and write by his mother. He worked in the bush at Tallawudjah and us kids were always overjoyed to see him when he came home to us.

Mum, Sarah Jane Etta (Simpson), born on 5 November 1895 at Tallawudjah, was of a slight willowy build with a beautiful head of long, wavy auburn hair that she used to wear in a row of small buns at the nape of her neck. From time to time she used to suffer from debilitating, bilious headaches that she believed came from having long hair. She often asked Dad to cut her hair but he loved her long hair. One day, Dad gave in and cut it short and it remained like this for the rest of her life.

Prior to her marriage, Sarah Jane was living with her parents on their farm, south of Glenreagh, helping her family with the farming chores. Some of the farm paddocks were divided by Barkaway Creek trickling through the paddocks. This creek caused many of their farm animals to become bogged in the soft, muddy section of the creek while trying to get a drink. This happened one day to two cows when Sarah and her sister Lizzie were home alone.

This was in 1915, when the last connecting section of the railway coming north from Sydney, Coffs Harbour to Glenreagh, was being constructed across the Orara River from the Simpson farm. World War 1 was in its infancy and this connecting section of the railway was being cleared and prepared for the last section to be laid. Workmen were across the Orara River from my grandparent's farm doing this work.

Sarah and Lizzie decided to go over and seek help to get the cow out of the bog. This proved successful with two men lending a hand. When Sarah's father, Granddad Charles, came home he went over to thank the men. He invited them over for a meal the next Sunday night. Tom Holder, who was one of the men, came over for the meal and must have liked what he saw as he kept visiting - and he became my Dad.

Dad enlisted for World War 1 in 1916 and was given a farewell in Glenreagh. While overseas he corresponded with Mum. He was invalided home in late 1917, and he knocked on the Simpson's front door with an engagement ring in his pocket before Mum knew he was even back in Australia.

My parents went to live on Granny Simpson's farm at Tallawudjah Creek shortly after their marriage in Christ Church Glenreagh on the 3 July 1918.

My parents took over the old Simpson Property, known as Granny's farm, up the creek. This was a comfortable home for the family. Dad worked in the timber and Mum ultimately had a few cows for the future needs of us kids. My grandparents had planted many fruit trees when they first settled here with a grove of orange trees plus peach and pear trees. Lemon trees also grew close by and the creek banks were covered with wild blackberry bushes.

Tom & Sarah Holder - wedding 1918

In June 1919, twelve months after their marriage and being settled on Grandma Simpson's farm up Tallawudjah Creek, my eldest sister Daphne was born. Her birth however was unlike the early births of the pioneers up the creek who depended on assistance from their neighbours. She was born in Grafton and my father often recalled her birth as a strange time for him. After seeing his wife and the safe arrival of his daughter he had to get home. He had been at his sister's home in Queen

Street, Grafton. Due to the closure of many of the streets, because of the Spanish Flu pandemic that was happening at that time, he had difficulty finding his way to the punt service that operated over the Clarence River to South Grafton. He walked about 35 miles home to Tallawudjah – getting there the next morning.

L to R: Tom, Sarah holding baby Mac, Daphne, Charlie, Bessie, Uncle Jack Simpson with Agnes, 1925.

Dad had a saying all his life about working: *"A man needed to be there in daylight and home before dark."* Later on in his farming days, when our neighbour had put lights on his tractor so he could plough at night, my Dad still used to tell us that any man should be able to make a living between daylight and dark. Us kids used to smile to ourselves when in our teenage years we were farming north of Grafton on the Clarence River. He would light the lantern and asks us kids to come up into the barn with him to husk corn ready for the threshing contractor to come. He deemed that it wasn't work as he kept up his supply of stories, recitations and friendly advice to us on being neighbourly - as he always put it!

Timber Top, 1925, at the cave.

Dad had a bullock team early in our time at Tallawudjah and our parents told us in later years how we used to run and tell Mum that Smart and Dodger were coming up the lane - they were the names of Dad's leading bullocks. I know he was taking logs to Allan Taylor's Mill at Glenreagh. I later learned, after I returned to Glenreagh to live in 1982 and enjoyed many cards nights with Tom Chapman, that Dad also carted sleepers to the railway station at Glenreagh. Tom informed me that the cartage price was three pence (2 cents) per sleeper. I haven't been able to find out how many sleepers would make a load for a bullock team of 24 bullocks.

I feel sure the load would have been prepared the day before in readiness for the long slow trip to the railway station the

Tom Holder's bullock team crossing Tallawudjah Creek in 1929 with a 100ft ironbark pole on the wagon.

next day. They would have travelled on what was known as the Back Road to Glenreagh (now Shipmans Road). From our home, Tallawudjah Creek Road at that time crossed the creek five times before it forked to the left and went down past the school to again cross the creek. It then went along the flat past Hoosen's and crossed the creek once more. This is where the Bridge is now and has been for many years. This road was known back then as the Long Way to Glenreagh. The Back Road forked to the right and was a much shorter trip to the station. This is the road that the bullockies took with their teams, as well as any people riding horses.

Dad still had his bullock team after our family moved into their new home next door to the Simpson farm in 1928. He was able to carry on with his bullock team, snigging logs out of his back paddock to the railway siding at Timber Top. They would be loaded onto railway trucks and sent to the mill at Glenreagh for processing.

Road worker's camp at the Junction, with fallen tree

About 1933-34 a road gang came to live in tents at Avery's Creek, as the junction at Tallawudjah was then called. They were assigned to build a new road from the upper reaches of Tallawudjah Creek to where it connected at the 1260 turn off, then onto the old road. This went a short distance before diverting behind Horace Shipman's residence to once more join the existing road on the western side of the creek, crossing near where the Tallawudjah Creek School once stood. While this planned, and in due course executed, road took away eight creek crossings from the road traveller, it caused great anguish to my Dad. He rode his horse many miles to try and get the problem resolved without success. The new road, when it came, would completely cut off the creek water supply for all our cattle. No natural water supply at all. The new road when built would come between the dairy and our home

Fortunately, when the road gang first came, they camped at the Junction. They came from building a road at Bucca Creek with all their camping gear on a truck. By afternoon they had their tents erected just past the creek crossing. A decision was made to cut a tree down that appeared to be too close to their tents. But to their surprise, it fell across the newly erected tents. This caused some amusement among the timber workers who lived along the creek.

The new road, showing the old road and Tallawudjah Creek.

I well remember they all went home for their Christmas holidays after being there a short time. They had been to our place and had some fun on the tennis court, so when most of them came back to work, they had bought a new tennis racquet each. All of these road workers were from the coal fields area around Kurri Kurri and Cessnock. They were mine workers, but for some reason that I can't remember, they were out of work and were put to work building roads through some government scheme.

They were a great addition to the fun we had both on the tennis court and at the parties as they joined in everything. As the road came closer to our farm they shifted their camp quite close to our home and enjoyed our swimming hole during the warmer months.

These men supported functions in both Glenreagh and Nana Glen and formed many lifelong friendships with our family. In fact, one of them became a family member when he married my eldest sister Daph. Others visited us with their families many years later after we had moved from Glenreagh.

Tom retired with pet cow, Grafton 1948

Our Mum and Dad both had a unique way of making our Christmas holidays special – Dad used to remind us to be good and make sure Mum had plenty of wood in the kitchen because Santa knows when we are good. He would then go on to remind us of what we had not done or when one of us had been unkind. My earliest memory of my Dad was he was a fun man who loved his wife and kids.

Mum had come from a farming background and she already had a couple of cows that she was milking for our needs. The nearest shop was over ten miles away and all the women of that era were well trained in organising their food supplies. Flour was purchased in 50lb bags and sugar in 70lb sacks. The pantry shelf at the end of the kitchen was always well stocked with jams and preserves.

The pressure of living and creating a loving home for their family didn't seem to be a chore to my parents as they set about getting their growing family to school. Besides being husband and wife, they were good mates, and supported each other in every way. I recall asking Dad something one day and he just said, "Oh, I think we had better go and ask your Mum about this". He walked with me, his hand on my shoulder, while the question was discussed to find a solution.

Mum took the washing to the creek. A line was hung from tree to tree nearby and it was easier to take the clean clothes home than to carry water from the creek. I do not remember a bathroom in Granny's home but I do recall the old round wash tubs being placed in front of the open fire and us kids having a bath, sometimes two kids at the same time.

Washing days were great fun for us kids as we happily skipped stones across the water and carried buckets or billies full of water to the tubs to help Mum. My parents had a great way of involving all the family in helping, no matter what the job was.

I did not know what my parents were deciding to do about our situation on the property at Tallawudjah. The new road was coming closer, and when my Granny died in June 1936, and shortly after her share farmer left the Glenreagh farm, the decision was made to take our cows over to her farm. Mum and the kids would do the milking while Dad stayed at the creek for the time being to care for things there. The milking job was much larger on Granny's Glenreagh farm but an adult cousin came to help. Dad used to ride his horse over every week-end and ride back with his weekly food supply until Granny's affairs were settled.

That is when my family left Tallawudjah Creek. We still owned the property but at that time there was a greater need at my grandparent's property. We ultimately sold our property and moved to farm at Southgate on the Clarence River in August 1938.

It wasn't the first time that I had lived with Granny Simpson. My dear grandfather Charles Simpson had died in 1931. My Mum had lost our baby sister Joan in 1934 and my Uncle Bill was killed felling timber at Sherwood in 1933. Uncle Bill, a bachelor, lived with his Mum, my Granny, on the Simpson farm at Glenreagh.

Sarah Holder, 1960

Mum was concerned for her mother living alone and sent me over to live with my Granny and attend school at Glenreagh. Many other cousins came to stay with us on the farm. Granny shared many history stories with me. She also made sure I learned to sew, but she had a strict rule that there was no sewing on a Sunday. I was always making dolls clothes, and she repeatedly told me that I would have to pick all the stitches out with my nose when I died if I sewed on Sundays. She caught me several times up under the bed - sewing. It was a rather lonely life and Sundays were for going to church and remaining in your 'going out clothes' ready for family visitors to visit. It was a day of worship and rest.

When I was with her, she was picked up by the Rector in his car as he came from Nana Glen to Glenreagh. After church he would drive us back home where she served him with a hot meal before he left for other services throughout the valley. There was no electricity so how did she do it? There was no one at home to keep the fire going, but go it did.

Granny Elizabeth sat in her chair in the front room every night – no lounge room in that era. Near her chair was a small three-legged cane type table that held the large family bible. Every night she would read a short passage or just a few lines from it to me, always just before 8 pm, then as the clock struck eight o'clock she would say, "Eight the clock is striking ma, may I go out? For my love is waiting for to take me out!".

And with that she would whisk me away to bed. I slept in a room by myself and she always made sure I was tucked in but was not the kissing type but sometimes patted me. She seemed pleased that I was the only grandchild named after her. I am sure I was blessed in sharing this time with Granny. I thank her for my love of history as she talked about life as it was for her and neighbours in those early days of settlement in this area we now cherish.

I missed my family. After some twelve months my Grandmother Elizabeth's youngest daughter came to work on the farm with her husband and two school aged boys, and live in the second home. I returned to see out my school days at Tallawudjah Creek, leaving school when I was fourteen years old.

I have included the following two stories about Dad as they have stayed with me all my life.

The first story is about Dingoes.

Dad told us kids that the way to tell the difference between a dog and dingo was to check the scalp hair, as a dingo has 2 different scalp hairs. I don't know the truth of this as my memory of this fact might be a little hazy.

Dad was known as a good shot with either shotgun or rifle. He often earned an extra quid or two in those days as a shooter, as it was the depression years and every extra shilling mattered.

Many dingoes were roaming throughout the bush causing great anguish to the farmers. The dingoes used to come very close to our home at night and would kill any of our young calves. They became such a threat that Dad built a small paddock close to our home in an effort to keep our calves safe.

I can remember us kids laying in our beds, scared and covered in goose bumps, as the dingoes roamed in packs, howling outside our home. In the real bad times, Dad would get us to set fire to old tree stumps anywhere nearby to frighten the dingoes off. This action helped us to understand how to think and act positively when we are challenged.

I remember Dad occasionally getting a fox, but not often, as they were an introduced animal.

He would take any old, sick and aged cattle and drive them up a gully on our property to be shot. The animals were then skinned and the hide was thickly salted, folded into a package, about two feet square, and tied in place with fencing wire. Cured animal hides were then made ready for dispatch, with any other animal hides, to hide buyers in Sydney at Winchcombe Carson.

After the animal carcases had mostly decomposed, Dad would use them as a lure for poisonous baits that were set out for dingoes. Dad used strychnine baits for the dingoes and he would prepare them in his shed at home. We would ride our horses to any carcass and carefully lay the baits around, either on flat stones or on pieces of bark, and always with a stick to secure the baits. It was critical to ensure there was no skin contact, something that Dad was very careful to educate us kids about. I often went with him as he carefully counted the baits that were laid out.

Dad was always very careful about setting these baits, waiting until the birds went to roost, and always back at the carcass before daylight to pick up any uneaten baits. He would then search for any dead dingoes. He would skin a 4 or 6 inch strip from the dingo's head and take the tail as well as proof of a dingo kill. He would then peg out these skin pieces on the side of his shed at home to dry, using small inch nails located fairly close together to stretch the skin. Each proof of a dingo sent in would earn him five shillings at that time and I witnessed him skinning nine dingoes one morning.

The second story is about Flying Foxes.

There was a large camp of flying foxes over the mountain area from our home in the general direction of Kangaroo Creek. They were causing some concern around the whole area, attacking all kinds of fruit trees and being real pests with their presence and smell.

A party of shooters from Glenreagh and Tallawudjah Creek, including my parents, were encouraged by the PPU Board to try and reduce their numbers. I think PPU stood for the Pastures Protection Union. The PPU supplied the ammunition free for the shooters. Mum went along to snip the claws off the dead flying foxes as the shooters were paid two pence for each pair of claws.

Dad, ever the resourceful man, really liked the orange colour on the flying foxes and decided to help himself to some skins plus some of the contrasting colour on their bodies. He had tanned wallaby rugs for all us kids to put beside our beds so we could stand upon them on winter mornings as we dressed. Floor boards were cold to our feet.

Dad set about with these small oblong pieces of flying fox fur to see if he could tan them for a rug. He first set up his big tanning drum down by the edge of the creek, on the stone area, so the fire wouldn't get away, and mixed up his tanning mixture. I know he used wattle bark but I don't recall what else. Us kids were marshalled to keep the fire burning and had a stick to stir the contents of the drum from time to time.

He had a rough type bench structure nearby and from time to time he would have us join him to scrub the fur with flat stones to get any flesh off. I can't re-call how many times the skins were placed back into the tanning mixture but I do recall that there always appeared to be a big armful of wattle bark laying at the side of the fire.

Dad continued to wash and scrub those skins but he couldn't seem to dim the strong flying fox smell, in other words, they smelt terrible. He tried all kinds of things in the wattle bark mixture until he tried scented soap and bingo, it worked.

He was delighted and set about drying and cutting the skins to size. They were rectangular in shape, about 4 or 5 inches long by about 2 1/2 inches wide. Mum sewed them together on her old Singer sewing machine using two rows of orange colour and then two rows of contrast. It grew into a double bed size rug which she backed with a soft orange colour material.

It was on display at the Grafton Show and it caused a lot of interest. The show committee asked if my parents would send it up to the Brisbane show. When they agreed, Mum took the Official's advice and backed the rug with a heavier contrast colour, which improved its appearance.

The rug was a feature in my parent's bedroom for many years. By the time us kids grew up, married and left home, it was showing signs of wear. We noticed that it was relegated to a rug for the sulky.

When we came back to live in Glenreagh in November 1982, there were no flying foxes around or even spoken about until the summer of 1994, when a mob of them set up camp in the trees on the banks on the Orara River. They have been fairly regular visitors to this same area since then.

After we came back here to live, I renewed acquaintances with my old school mates and was asked quite a few times about the flying fox rug. Questions like, did we still have it?

Sadly, I was living some 500 miles away when Mum and Dad retired from where we were farming at Southgate to live in Grafton. WWII was still on and I don't recall any word of where this special rug ended up.

Severe drought on Tallawudjah Creek - the big swimming hole used by workers. It was a very hot day and when the loaded bullock team came over the rise and saw the pool of water, they rushed for a drink and bogged the wagon in the loose gravel. Mum was always ready with her camera!

5. Us Kids

I am one of six children born to my Mum and Dad.

My eldest sister Daphne (Daph) was born in June 1919, my only brother Charles (Charlie) in December 1920 and I arrived in May 1922. A sister Agnes (Agie) was born in April 1924 and then Mildred (Mac) on her brother Charles' birthday, 7th December 1925.

On 5th December 1931 our baby sister Joan Mary Holder was born. Sadly she died aged 2 years and two months in 1934 from complications received from whooping cough. We three younger kids also had this complaint at the time but we recovered. With her older siblings to attend to her needs, Joan was a delight to everyone in our family. My Dad taught her the song 'When It's Springtime in the Rockies' and she used to sing it at house parties. Dad gave us all special songs when we were small, with Agie and I singing 'Two Little Girls in Blue' regularly.

We were all born in nursing homes in Grafton before we came home, mostly to Granny Simpson's old home at Tallawudjah. Baby Joan was the only one of us kids to come home to our new home that Dad had built for his family.

Granny's home at Tallawudjah was a very comfortable one. Dad at that time worked in the timber industry, and Mum had a few cows and of course a vegetable garden, as they set about raising their family.

We lived on this property for nearly ten years and as kids we were well known as 'Daph, Charlie and the three Holder kids'. I think this came from folk not being able to tell we three younger ones apart. I was a skinny little kid then and I guess we all looked the same, so you wore the title as one of the Holder kids.

Travelling merchants visited from time to time.

The public road went through our property and there were slip rails across this road near our home. We were told by our parents to let the rails down for anyone who was passing through. This was especially so for any teamsters as usually the bullocky was walking near the rear of his team and it assisted him greatly when, *'One of the Holder kids let the slip rails down'*.

My grandparents had planted a grove of orange trees plus many other fruit trees some years before we arrived and we benefited from this fresh fruit. There was a grove of some eight or ten orange trees, several china pear trees, a lemon and mandarin tree, and a huge mulberry tree. I can recall when we played or went for a walk each of us kids always had a bottle of orange juice to quench our thirst as we explored in the bush. Other times we roamed around the shallow creek that bounded the property, picking blackberries from the large bushes on the creek banks. We all walked with a billy tied with a bit of rope around our waists so that we could take some fruit home for our Mum. A warm blackberry pie smothered in cream…..yum!

Mum had us kids digging the garden and carrying water from the creek at every chance. She could grow anything and prided herself on seeing how many veggies she could get on our plates for Christmas dinner. I well remember there were 9 different vegetables on our plates one year.

Another thing I recall were the great discussions about egg settings. Visiting Aunts and women folk friends would discuss settings set by the fullness of the moon and of course there were many egg settings exchanged from one to the other as better egg layers were discussed.

I do not recall anyone butchering their own cattle. There was a butcher in Glenreagh but that was a long way for us to travel from where we lived up the creek. Any meat we did have was kept in a meat safe, as there was no other cooling or freezing method. Usually this was outside under the shade of a tree, in an airy meat safe. In hot summers, it would be corn beef or on special occasions a chook from the farm yard would be prepared for a sumptuous meal.

Mum kept our butter in the creek that was close to our home, hanging in a tin dangling in the water. There were fish in the creek and we had chooks, turkeys and geese for special occasions. I remember pigeon soup loaded with vegies being a regular meal followed by milk puddings or huge boiled puddings. Jam Roly polies were another treat as they were always served with custard. We loved it when Mum was away and Dad made us doughboys or spotted dogs, lovely and

Holder family c.1934 on rock at Talluwadjah Creek, from L to R: Sarah, Agnes, Jean Shipman, Bessie, 'Mac' and Daphne.

warm, and covered in butter and dripping with honey that he had robbed from nearby hives.

I remember the large fireplace in this old kitchen, where the fire always seemed to be alight. A sturdy back log just simmered away during the daylight hours. The back wall of this old kitchen was made of upright slabs of timber that seemed to just stand on their end. Inside the cracks in the walls were papered over to keep out the draught and the walls were whitewashed inside. This paper from time to time would get discoloured by the smoke and would either be whitewashed or covered with another upper layer. Us kids would sit around the fireplace and have fun making shadowy shapes on the walls with small fingers while Dad told stories.

There was a long landing that went from the verandah outside the kitchen door into the bedroom section of the home. At the back of the kitchen were the wash tubs, with just loose boards laid down on the dirt as a base to walk on.

Holder family in 1961, the same on rock at Talluwadjah Creek, from L to R: Sarah, Bessie Webb and children Robyn, Lynece, Peter (front).

The kitchen, a happy place, had a strong beam fastened overhead with cast iron cooking pots or a smaller kettle hanging from long chains. One chain in particular, held an ever boiling fountain of water, always on the boil for anyone passing by to have a cuppa. I recall one frequent visitor was a man named 'Cold Tea Bill' because he didn't mind if the tea already in the pot was a bit cold.

In later years, when my Mum was ill and I was looking after her she spoke often about that period of her life. She spoke of the way my Dad used to come home from his days in the bush and would always assist her to feed the family. Early on there were five of us kids with the eldest being seven years old.

Mum would have us washed and in our night attire ready for our evening meal. After Dad tidied himself, as he called it, they would set about making sure we were all fed. There were no special baby chairs for us, we either sat on cushions on ordinary chairs or the smallest on either of our parent's knee.

Then Dad would 'piggy-back' the little ones, telling stories of course, as they went across the landing that separated the kitchen from the bedroom section of the home. This was designed in many of the older homes as an attempt to save the sleeping section of the home in case of a fire in the kitchen where the open fire mostly burnt all day long. Afterwards, Mum and Dad would sit together and enjoy their evening meal in peace.

Bessie in 1923.

In remembering my formative years, my most vivid memory is of clinging to my brother Charlie's back, as he piggy backed me when I was little. He was always there for me. Our parents always instilled in us to look after one another, especially caring for the younger ones.

When I arrived I think my eldest sister Daph was mostly helping Mum so Charlie was given the responsibility of looking after me. One time I can remember Mum wanting some lemons from the tree in the orchard so she asked Charlie to go down and get some for her. He took me with him - Why did he do this? He placed me under the tree while he threw stones up to try and knock some lemons down. Yes, one stone came down on my foot and cut it badly. He piggy backed me home for Mum to fix it up.

Mum had a fair gaggle of geese and it was Charlie's job to pen them up at night. The story goes that I, as a toddler, always went with him. The gander always took to me and bit me anywhere he could. I would come home crying with bruises and bite marks on me. Dad would tell Charlie that it was his job to look after his little sister and protect her from the gander. (Thinking about it now, why didn't they just keep me at home out of harm's way?). One night Charlie took a nice sized stick with him and the story goes that when the gander came at me, Charlie flattened him with a sturdy knock on the head and said, "I put him to bed, Dad". After Dad realised the gander was dead, his quick response was to get the gander ready and prepared for eating. No food source was wasted in those days!

Bessie - 10 months old.

I don't recall any parts of these two stories. I was much too young but my Dad used to take great delight in telling us kids about the things we did when we were little. Today, I remember fondly the bond that my brother and I had all our lives that was formed as kids nearly 100 years ago.

We were happy there and all us kids had happy memories of our childhood. I don't know the reason why my parents bought the property next door and built their own home there. It was going to be a little closer to the school that had opened in 1927. That may have been the reason as it would save about half a mile and two crossings of the creek that intertwined with the roadway on the walk to school.

Maybe, they knew my Grandparents, who still owned the farm, were nearing the end of their lives and this would mean the property would likely be sold.

Growing up for me, even in our new home, seemed to take a long time. My older sister and brother had left school and were attending social functions in Glenreagh. I was about to leave school, as my 14th birthday was fast approaching, and I was keen to explore beyond Tallawudjah.

Our parents had always either taken or encouraged us to attend church. We didn't always attend because of wet weather and having to ride horses the long distance to Glenreagh. It was decided it was time for me to accompany my brother Charles so we both could be confirmed. This was a commitment of 12 months, to learn and prepare for confirmation, that took place on 5 October 1935 in Christ Church Glenreagh. I had been baptised in this same church on 3 September 1922.

For 12 months we rode into the little church that I have had a strong connection with. My grandparents had helped to build it, my Grandad was the first Warden and my Auntie Annie was the first bride married in the church on 24 June 1914. I have been a regular church goer to this little timber church since returning to Glenreagh. Recently, I celebrated my baptism of 101 years ago on 3 September 2023, in this important building.

1961 - Three generations standing on the original house back step from 1928, the home having been removed to Timber Top.
L - R: Sarah Holder, Bessie Webb and daughter Robyn Webb.

6. Our New Home

*E*ven at my age now I still remember the day we shifted into our new home.

Dad had a draft horse and cart while Mum had the sulky to shift all our possessions from Granny's home to our new home, with Daph and Charlie helping them. We three younger ones, Agie, Mac and me, all under 6 years old, were allowed to walk the distance from Granny's home and carry our dolls. We were given a severe warning about being careful when we were crossing the creek as we had to cross it twice, even though our new home was on the next property to Granny's. Part of the clothing from Mac's doll fell into the running water and was soon on its way into the deeper water of the creek. Mac, crying, took off trying to get to it but Agie and I grabbed her and held her back. We had been taught by our parents, all our short lives, to look after the younger ones. Over the many decades of my life I have often thought about Mum and Dad's teachings and the influence it had on me as I raised my own children.

Holder's new home, 1928.

Dad built our new home on the property that he now owned, with assistance from his friend from Glenreagh, Harry Dun. With the bedroom section of our new home finished in 1928, the moving day finally arrived. Initially it was a four room building with a hallway that went through separating the bedrooms. It had three bedrooms at the front, a front and back verandah and a front room that today we call a living room or lounge.

It was certainly an adventure for us kids to shift into our new home. We had so much more room as the four girls shared two of the bedrooms. Daph the oldest with Mac the youngest, were in one bedroom. Agie and me, the two middle aged ones, were in the other bedroom. My brother Charlie had an area for himself in the front room and Mum and Dad had their bedroom.

The new home faced east with a front verandah and was some seven steps high at the front and it was close to the roadway at the front. There was also a verandah with the ends closed in, facing west at the back. Steps went down off this verandah on the northern end into a bark galley where Mum did the cooking for some time until Dad was able to get the kitchen built.

It was from this home that I commenced school on 29 May 1928, my sixth birthday.

Later Dad built our new kitchen with a new verandah that joined the existing back verandah and this space formed a sizable space for many parties and dances as our family grew. It had the dimensions of a small hall. This section he left open-ended as a kind of breeze way. It was always open in summer but Dad had canvas blinds made to close the ends in to make it warmer for winter. Mum played the piano and my Uncle Charlie the accordion and this space was great for dances and parties.

Bessie with her dog, kitchen in background, 1930.

The kitchen itself was Dad's pride and joy. At the southern end was the bathroom and walk in pantry. However, it was the fireplace that people came to see as it was the centre piece of our new home. The huge fireplace was 13 sheets of iron wide. The fireplace area was raised some 6 inches higher than the kitchen floor. At one end a fuel stove plus space for wood to be stacked stood on the smooth concrete floor. At the other end was space for a big open fire defined by the rim from a sulky or coach wheel with concrete surrounding it. There was room for us kids to sit between it and the stove while others sat in front of the open fire on chairs on the kitchen floor.

I remember sitting around this fire, especially on winter nights, plucking feathers from the birds being prepared for a nourishing meal the next day, or shelling cobs of corn which were used to feed the poultry. During drought periods corn was fed to some of the older bullocks in nosebags made from sugar bags.

Dad would be telling us stories, with Mum always busy in the kitchen between ironing, sewing, or cooking. A little later Dad had a water tank installed with a tap through to the kitchen which made life easier for Mum. In winter, when I was little, it was where we all bathed one after the other in the same water in front of the fire. Mum had her work table at that end of the kitchen and the tap was quite close to it. On that side of the home she had a huge fenced in area that was her vegetable garden and it was here that she excelled.

On other nights Dad would sit us around the table and teach us to play cards, especially cribbage, as he thought that would assist us with our school work. Both my parents were keen card players but were very much against gambling.

I especially remember the card parties. I also remember Dad purchasing a battery powered wireless to hear the cricket Tests that were being played in England. Neighbours came to play cards and to hear the scores. As the kids went to sleep, they were put down to sleep, several in the same bed.

Dad built a tennis court on the other side of the road from the front of the home and folk used to ride their horses over from Back Creek to play tennis on Saturday afternoons, have a party at night and then play again the next morning before riding home ready for work on Mondays. Thinking now about how people of that era enjoyed themselves can be expressed best by, 'The simple things of your life were improved if you

Holder's new home with tennis court and road in foreground -
taken from Dun's property across the creek, 1928.

had something, then the joy of sharing it with your neighbours made everything better.'

Building the new home where Dad did meant we had two creek crossings less to get anywhere. It did mean a shorter distance to travel to the Glenreagh village for church and supplies. Also, a shorter distance for the kids to walk to school.

I remember that Dad built our tennis court in 1928. He was very busy lining the court one morning ready for a tennis afternoon, with visitors coming, when there was a huge storm and the court was completely covered by flood waters in the afternoon. Old timers spoke about that flood for years with tales of a cloud burst.

This flood carried about a metre length small log and it came to rest on the top of a large stump that was in a nearby paddock and Mum took a photo to prove the height of that flood. The stump was a fair way away from the creek bed and it was surprising to folk to witness the stranded log years after.

Our Holder home and tennis court were the scene of many happy times. There was a piano in the walled in section of our home and my Mum and older sister, Daphne both played it. My Uncle Charlie played the squeeze box and my Dad recited at every occasion. Any visitors were encouraged to perform and they often did. Mum encouraged us kids to sing and I can recall singing "Springtime in the Rockies" with my sibling.

There were a few sleeper cutters camping near our new home. As we were milking house cows and making our own butter, we helped them out with these, if it was needed. I recall Mum used to cook their corned meat for some of them. There were great friendships made and these timber men, as we kids called them, would look out for us kids if Mum or Dad were called away on some emergency. When we had card nights and socials in this home they were welcome to attend.

They sometimes went home for weekends. I remember one man came from near Kempsey. He brought my Mum a carnival ware sugar basin as a gift for cooking his corned beef and the basin is still in our family. It is known as Jim Jebb's sugar basin. Unfortunately, it is recorded in the Glenreagh cemetery records that Jim is buried there, having died on 4 August 1933. His grave is unmarked but his parents are noted as James and Elizabeth Jebb.

It was about 1930 when Dad decided to take up dairying as an occupation for his growing family. The house cow population had grown and us kids had learnt to help Mum milk the house cows. We also loved rearing the little calves.

Dad swapped his bullocks for his friend Fred Green's cows. A cow yard and dairy were built by Dad, he purchased a hand turned separator and was soon in business. This move also meant that Dad didn't have to go into the bush every day, and we were still managing the farm section of Granny's farm.

Dad was ploughing and planting corn and other crops, and I recall one very large paddock that he had planted with turnips. Us kids had to walk behind his horse and dray, pulling the turnips out of the ground for Dad to feed his pigs.

He was always engaging us kids in his plans. Was it on purpose - his way of teaching us to be responsible?

Dad also needed to build a separate cream dairy. This was a small building situated between the cow yard, dairy and the house. It had a concrete floor that went up some 10 or 12 inches high at the edges. It held some water and the cream cans stood in this until delivery day, which in winter was two days weekly and summer three days. Above the concrete on the walls a strip of some 8 to 10 inches of gauze mesh went around the building to let the cool night air circulate. This was to keep the cream as cool as possible and to also cool any freshly separated cream, before it was added to the can.

The Milk Carter came from the Cream Factory at Coramba and met the Creek farmers on the road across the creek past the school. My eldest sister Daphne used to take our supply in the sulky and she would pick up Arold Shipman's cream as she drove past their roadside dairy on her way to the meeting place.

Dad was happy to let his wife and kids do the dairy while he still worked in the timber. Friends told me in later years that he was an expert on advising younger timber workers how many sleepers they could expect to cut from any particular tree before it was felled. Having lived in the bush all his life he had an eye for the heights and girths of the trees.

In recalling those early days of my family commencing their farming pursuits, I can well remember the morning my brother Charlie cut his foot. It was his job to get the cows rounded up and in the yard, and Mum's and my job to milk them while Charlie made a fire to get the water hot, ready for the cleaning up process of the dairy utensils.

While chopping some wood, he cut his foot badly from his big toe up his foot towards his ankle. A quick rush for Mum to get bandages for the cut and another one for me and my younger sister to get our sulky horse caught, harnessed and ready for a hurried trip. Dad was already in the bush at his work, and I recall my eldest sister, whose job it was to take care of the younger kids, helping Agnes and me to harness the horse with Joan the baby sitting up in her arms. The foot was heavily bandaged and raised up on a butter box in the sulky as Mum took off to drive to Jack Shipman's place to phone for the ambulance to come and take Charlie to Grafton hospital.

She went on to meet the ambulance at Glenreagh, while us kids finished the milking chores at home. The older ones took care of the younger ones, as we were taught all our lives to do: to love one another and to take care of one another.

I don't know why my parents wanted to buy and build next door to Granny's place. Perhaps it was that they knew Granny's place would have to be sold as my grandparents were getting on in years. They were no longer working their own place at Glenreagh as they had share farmers in for years. Whatever the reason for Dad building our new home, it was a special place for us kids.

The home being high off the ground at the front meant there was a lovely cool area for us kids to play in the dirt under the house. We used to make our own wagons out of cotton reels for logs and we also used the core of a cob of corn. We would make roads, bridges and water holes and just do what our fathers did, take our imagery timber logs to the mill. If the mood struck us we would often wander off into the bush or down to the creek and float our home made stick boats.

Dad had a very shrill whistle and Mum had a co-ee call and we knew to answer either call and come home promptly.

As we grew older the tennis court, that Dad had built while he was working on the house, was a great place to keep us kids close to the home as two or four could play, and we often did.

Picnic & tennis day at Arold Shipman's court.

Dad was very strict about us playing fair. We wouldn't be on the court very long before there would be words going back and forward about whether the ball was in or out. Dad who was usually working in the shed close by or sitting on the verandah reading his paper, would whistle us off the court and give us a talking too about playing fair and not arguing. He would then tell us to sit and think about it. After some ten minutes or so we would ask if we could go back on the court. He would always ask if we were ready to play fair, and of course we said yes.

Group on tennis court - Holder family (Tom with cap)
with Shipman familes and others.

We wouldn't be back on the court for about ten minutes before we would be having the same 'to-do' as he called it. He always used to add that when we got cranky with one another we couldn't think properly. A good tennis player doesn't get crabby. I wouldn't know how many times he had this patience with us, but teach us he did, and he never seemed to give in to us.

Mum played tennis and Dad didn't at this time, but he did learn later and had the reputation of being a very heady player.

I don't remember celebrating any Christmas days in Granny's house but I can recall several that we enjoyed in our new home. One in particular was when Dad and Mum had moved their bed out into the breezeway on the verandah, into the end that had been enclosed some months before Christmas.

Dad would repeatedly be telling us kids that we had better think about the jobs we were doing, mainly for Mum, like carrying water from the creek for her garden, and his pet one, keeping the wood box full so she didn't have to go and get it. He would then proceed to tell us that Santa knew all about the times we were cranky with one another and he would always drop in something about how good he and Mum had been.

As Santa had to walk past his bed he thought he would put up a chaff bag, and he would get all our presents. He would then remind us of several things or times that we were cross or naughty until we were all in doubt around Santa time we would receive any presents.

Holder children, Christmas 1930. L-R: Daphne, Charlie, Bessie, Agnes, Mac

How we laughed Christmas morning when all Dad had in his chaff bag was a carpenter's pencil. We danced around him, laughing, as he told us "that he supposed he was greedy, expecting a big bag full when there were so many kids to go around".

I remember that some of the kids from school tried to tell our family that there was no Santa Claus and we wouldn't hear of it. We argued the point back and went on to tell them how Dad nearly caught him once at our home.

This was another Christmas. Just before dawn Dad ran through our home ringing a cowbell, calling out help. We were bigger kids then but we still had our pillow cases on the foot of our beds and Santa had already been to our bedrooms. My eldest sister, Daph, slept in one of the bedrooms at the front of the home and we thought that we nearly caught Santa that morning as he didn't have time to go into her room with her presents. He had dropped them on the mat at the door as Dad was chasing him. She was a teenager and she had received a lovely underwear set.

It was such a joy back then for young ladies to get shop bought underwear. I remember she was very happy about her present as we younger ones thought we nearly caught Santa that night-time.

Holder children after church, 1936. L-R: Daphne, Charlie, Bessie, Agnes, Mac

7. Aunty Milda and Uncle Jack

As we settled into our new home our family life changed a little. My Uncle Jack had married; he was my Mum's brother and he had wed my Dad's sister, our Auntie Mildred known as Aunty Milda. Us kids knew them well as Uncle Jack had lived with us for some time in the old Simpson home while he was buying and building his own home further up the Creek. Aunty Milda used to come down from 'The Washpool' to mind us kids every time there was a new baby coming into our home. The practise was for new mothers to prepare a week or two for the new baby's arrival in South Grafton. Or over in Grafton, depending on where relatives lived or where the nursing homes they were booked into were located. I know I was born at Nurse McKnight's nursing home in South Grafton.

My cousin Rexie John Simpson, my Uncle and Aunty's first child, was born in April 1929.

A strong bond between our two families developed, now living some two miles apart using the old road route, as they settled into improving their property at the far end of the creek.

Two years later in 1931, when it was raining and the creeks were up Uncle Jack arrived at our home with Rexie, a toddler, for us kids to mind. He quickly returned home taking my Mum with him while Dad rode his horse to Jack Shipman's home to phone for medical help.

When Dad came back, he told Charlie and me where the creek, now in moderate flood, would be easier to cross for the Doctor, who would be coming soon to bring Aunty Milda a baby. In due course he arrived and we confidently showed him the best course of action to take, he gave us some lollies, and he went under our watchful eye across the creek. As he progressed midstream he lifted his medical bag a little higher out of flood reach. This caused Charlie to advise me that it was to keep the baby dry. The innocence of youth in that era! Dad, with a grin, would often remind us of this story when we were older and we had found out where babies do come from.

Uncle Jack's bark hut

Sadly, Aunty's little baby girl only survived 17 hours and had passed away by the time the Doctor had arrived at their place. Dad and Uncle Jack carried my Aunty on a home-made stretcher made with poles threaded through chaff bags to get Aunty to the ambulance. The stretcher rested on their shoulders as they walked around the hills to avoid the swollen creeks. The little baby was carried in a cane picnic basket that had a lid. They stopped at our home on the way, and I remember Dad opening the lid and showing us the little bub that looked like she was just sleeping.

My parents were always very thoughtful about our family visiting Uncle Jack's place. I think it was because they were developing it and there were jobs to be done with Dad helping and Aunty Milda always having jobs for us kids. They had a high wire netting fence around their home. Inside the fence, beside the vegetable garden in one area, there was a lawn where several young wallabies either grazed or rested. Aunty used to get us to put out food in tins for all kinds of animals and sometimes birds as well. Anything that was orphaned she rescued and fed. Aunty's home and surroundings were as clean as could be. Us kids were asked to pick up the tins after the animals were all fed and we then washed and wiped them clean so that they were ready for the next time.

Aunt Matilda with son Rex, born 1929

Wallabies were sometimes killed for dog food as the butcher was some 10 to 12 mile away. Sometimes a small Joey would be in the pouch and it would be bottle fed. I remember Aunty had a crow in a cage and my Uncle taught it to say some words and it also used to imitate people laughing. My Mum had a kind of slight squeal to commence her laugh and the crow used to imitate her. This would have Mum laughing all the louder and the crow as well.

Aunty Milda was a kind and caring lady to all that made up life in the bush surroundings. Her home was a delight to our eyes but she was careful that it was only eyes that saw her displays, not little fingers. She had a collection of bird eggs, but we were only allowed to take one egg from each nest that we found to add to the collection. She made us net bags on a handle to catch butterflies for her glass enclosed butterfly collection. In another corner of her front room was a lovely taller glass cage with a lifelike little blue wren sitting on a tree branch with a little jenny nearby on a small limb. The nest with eggs in it was so life like and real. My Aunty was a home taught taxidermist and she had done it all.

Another feature of her home, one that us kids were allowed to peep at from the door, was her lovely bedroom. Before their marriage, Uncle Jack had purchased a lovely four poster bed

Uncle Jack's home

from the great white train that had visited Glenreagh railway station in 1926. It was travelling around the rail network advertising and displaying samples of what Australian items could be purchased. On the bed was a white bedspread and on top of that was a lovely golden-shaded, tanned dingo hide. The hide even had marbles inserted for his eyes and it mesmerised us kids as we peeped from the doorway.

Aunty Milda used to make her own bread and I remember Uncle Jack made Blackberry wine. I don't know what it tasted like. He also made another one from chillies.

Aunty was always very fussy about her toilet. It was well away from the home and it was called the long drop style. She got my Uncle to make two different size holes, I guess because of their son Rex. At the side of the seat she had a narrow box built that contained ashes from the kitchen stove and users of the toilet were encouraged to put a scoop of ashes down the hole after any use of the toilet. Also, hanging from two nails near the ashes was two sizes of newspaper squares ready for use. I don't remember toilet paper back then, or perhaps it hadn't made its way into far flung bush locations.

My Uncle Jack was a hard worker and he toiled long hours on this property. He sadly died in his late fifties, like many folks of that era. Aunty Milda continued to work the farm with her son Rex until her passing some twenty years later.

Our family had left living as their neighbours in 1936 when we moved over to Glenreagh to manage Granny's farm. When it was sold we moved to live at Southgate on the Clarence River in 1938. In 1940 we had Rex visit us for a holiday with 'the kids' as he used to call us. We had a good time together.

When Les and I came back to Glenreagh to live in 1982 Rex, his wife Heather and family lived in Glenreagh. Rex still owned the Tallawudjah Creek farm. He was my first visitor and we straight away took up the friendship of those long ago childhood years. He visited me every day for a quick hello and chat over a cuppa, and I guess, to renew the family love we shared as kids growing up together. Sadly, he passed away suddenly at his home in 1988 and Heather and I shared a caring friendship for many years afterwards.

Holder family sitting on log cart at Uncle Jack's, 1925.
L-R: Sarah standing holding Agnes, Charlie, Tom with Bessie, Daphne.

8. My First School

First a little bit of history about how my first school was established.

A Progress Association was formed in 1891 at Tallawudjah Creek and a request for a half-time school was made. It opened in January 1892 and closed four years later, only to reopen later in that same year as a Provisional School. This meant that the school had more than twelve and less than twenty-five pupils. The parents were responsible for providing the school building and furniture with the Education Department arranging the teacher. Just two years later the school closed and once again reopened the same year, this time as a half-time School, staying that way until 1905. When it closed for four years, it meant the few children attending had to attend Glenreagh School, a distance of some miles away.

A half-time School reopened again in 1909, with Tallawudjah School and Boonjaub School, which was located about ten kilometres north of Glenreagh on the Grafton road. Mr F. Tully was the teacher. It was reported that the district was saddened when he was transferred to Bellingen in 1913 and over a hundred and fifty residents attended a musical evening with dancing to bid him farewell.

There were only three children going to the old Creek school, built with split slabs and a shingle roof, when it closed in 1912. They were Lizzie Simpson, Con Shipman and Jimmy Boldes and they then attended Glenreagh Primary School.

The teachers for this period were:

Angus Munro	1892
Alexander Moyes	1893
Josiah Gittens	1893
Ada Selman	1894
Louisa McPhee	1896
Albert H Munro	1898
J.McIntyre	1899
H. Hamilton	1900
H. McCauley	1901
P. Peard	1901
F. Cooper	1901
Mr O'Keefe	1902
F. Tully	1903
Ellis Small	1904
Bertie Swan	1911

Sadly, research found that Ellis Small passed away at Ulmarra in 1905 from the plague.

After many years a new school was sought as more people took up their holdings and the transient miners left the area, so there were more local children seeking an education.

A quote from Messrs. Milligan & Day for 336 pounds was accepted and the new school opened in 1927. Mr George Stevenson was the teacher, and it was at this one-teacher school that I joined my two older siblings on my sixth birthday on 29 May 1928.

In thinking about it now, I remember that I had recorded my first day at school for my eldest daughter Robyn, who had just received her first appointment to Llandilo Public School. She found herself with a class of forty two children, made up of kindergarten, first and second class aged children. I was driving the school bus at the time, taking the kids to and from school and I tried to assist her with stories to read to them as a whole class.

I was often called 'Bet-Bet' as a child.

Her very first day

A new school had been opened after many years of being without any education facility. This school wasn't very big. In fact, only one room and an entry porch. Many hooks were on the wall on one side and this is where the pupils hung their hats and school bags.

The desks were very long and would seat some 4 or 5 children. Bet-Bet was excited because it was her birthday, she was 6 and she had been given a pretty new crockery mug as a present. It had little girls holding hands and dancing all the way around it. Bet-Bet also received a pencil case with a painted picture on the lid. This lid caused a lot of interest as there was something to press and the lid rolled up like a blind. It caused a lot of excitement among the other children as no-one had ever seen anything like it – a snap back, roll up lid.

It was a long walk on the dusty dirt road, between 4 to 5 kilometres. We crossed the creek three times between our home and the school, meeting up with the two Shipman families on the way.

On her first day Bet-Bet became tired during the day and began to think of her home and her two younger siblings and her Mum. She started to cry. The teacher suggested she have a rest and she put her head on her arms on the desk and was soon asleep.

Bob Johnson was one of the bigger boys at school and he lived with his parents on the adjoining property to ours known as Dun's place. He often played with us. When school was over that first day Bob and Bet-Bet's big brother Charlie took it in turns to give her piggy-back rides on the way home.

When nearing home, they decided to rest near the creek bank. Bob told Charlie that he was there over the week-end and over near the big rock where the water was deep he thought he saw something. It was scary and the water was dark and it could have been a bunyip that the teacher had been reading about in the magazine story. Bob couldn't see it properly as a branch from the tree was leaning over the water.

Bet-Bet was sitting on the grass half asleep but heard the boys talking about bunyips. She thought…. what was a bunyip? No one had ever told her about a bunyip. She knew about the dangers of snakes and dingoes and going in deep water that her parents had taught her. But Bunyips, why hadn't someone told her before? Bob said it was scary and he carried a daisy air-gun! Was it a monster thing and would it grab anyone in the water if it was getting late.

The boys asked her, "Can you walk for a bit now as we had better get home?"

As Bob went through the gate to his place, a scared little girl almost ran the short distance to the safety of her home.

My school days had begun!

Mr George Stevenson was my first teacher but he wasn't there very long. I can't recall his face now but I remember he was kind to me.

Mr Ernest Chapman, a young teacher just out of College, was appointed in 1930. A young single man who in his retirement shared with me that he was ill equipped for the task that was before him on that first day. Whatever his fears he was well liked by both pupils and parents.

He boarded at the Glenreagh Hotel and rode a horse along the back road (now Shipmans Road) to Jack Shipman's property. He came down through it to a gate on the Long Road to Glenreagh, as it was then known, to another gateway just south of the school. There was a corner of the playground fenced off as a horse paddock.

It wasn't long before he was fondly referred to as "Chappie". He was keen on sport and was soon playing cricket and football for Glenreagh. He liked the one room school tidy and things in place. I recall a wood stove

'Chappie'

type fire in one corner but I don't ever recall the fire being lit for warmth. The top of the stove was used to store the large ink bottles that were used to fill up the small ink wells in the long desks that held four or five students.

I think we wrote with pencil until about third class.

Tallawudjah Creek school, 1930.

Chappie was very keen on commencing the morning classes with something mental for the whole school. There were two rows of desks with an aisle up the middle and he would ask questions to each section taking into consideration their ability. Firstly, as we marched in, we had to remain standing and if we got the question wrong, we had to sit down until there was only one student standing. Sometimes it was tables and other times just general knowledge or arithmetic, i.e., 'take-aways and additions'.

Now and again there would be a sheet of paper with money additions and even multiplication sums. This short contest amongst his pupils were eagerly contested by the older pupils and I expect a great learning experience to the younger ones.

Chappie was very fair minded and made sure we played a lot of sport. Because the pupils were small in number they all joined team games and played together under his watchful eye, and he even joined in to kick a ball when needed. In my latter years at school there was a tennis court.

We played 'Sheep, sheep come home' and 'Prisoner's Base'. Marbles was popular with everyone and we all seemed to have a bag of them.

The girls also played Hop-Scotch and Jacks.

The scary thing for me was the pit style toilets and they were labelled back then, Girls Lavatory and Boys Lavatory. One of the bigger boys received the cane for something that he did and threw the cane down the lavatory, but Chappie had a replacement laying in its place the next morning. I don't recall any other use of the cane at school.

Chappie took us roaming around the nearby paddocks and ploughed fields. We celebrated Arbour Day by always searching for different leaves and observing the roots on the different plants. When we went back to school we were encouraged to draw our specimens and press them. I recall the School Inspector being most impressed with our Nature Study books.

Chappie, also with the help of our parents, built a garden at the school. It was fenced in and he encouraged us to grow flowers from seed packets that he bought. In due course we were encouraged to plant them out to be colour co-ordinated and this was mainly done by the girls while the boys were helpful getting the manure from the horse paddock. When the flowers were in full bloom the girls were allowed to pick a bunch to take home to give to their mothers. Thinking of it now, it was a time each week when the whole school worked at a project together.

The school water supply was always a worry for Chappie. In Shipman's paddock, which was across the road from the school, lived an elderly man with quite a long beard who was well known locally, called 'Boy Scout'. He lived in two tent like structures and insisted on helping himself to the water supply at the school. There were two tanks and Boy Scout came regularly every afternoon with his two buckets to get his supply. He always carried two small pieces of board to put on the top of the full bucket of water to prevent spillage, so he would tell us kids. I remember one drought time Chappie suggested to him that he go to the nearby creek as the tanks were getting low and he was concerned for the children. His request fell on deaf ears as 'Boy Scout' continued his daily trip.

The creek wasn't very far from the school. A few times after an early storm, it wouldn't take much of a rise to put the creek up to a dangerous level too high for our little legs to cross. Some children lived on the school side of the creek, but the Symonds, Hoosons, Greens, William Bennett, Grays, Holders, H. Shipman's kids and Mavis Moran had to cross the creek. Chappie would saddle his horse and make sure we were all safely across before he rode home.

I remember us Holder kids would walk up to the Shipman's home with them on our way home. Mrs Elsie Shipman would give us dry clothes and something to eat before urging us on our way around the hill. Like our parents, we were warned to put a stick into any of the gullies to test the depth before we put our feet in the water to walk through. Mum was always relieved to see us coming out of the bush on the hill, often sometimes near dark. Normally the road from our place crossed over the creek three times on our way to school.

Chappie always enjoyed April Fool's Day and we kids had caught him out many times. The one trick we all remembered was when he caught out the whole school. We all arrived to find him quite excited and he had the school door shut.

He asked, "Would we put our bags down? Would the fastest runners stand by the door?" as a precaution. He had found a strange bird in the school room but had managed to put a box over it. We all went inside and he put us all around the box with the bigger kids ready to lift it and the rest to grab the

Chasing the Lolly Man at the school picnic, 1930.

bird. Tension rose as the box was slowly lifted under his tense guidance to reveal a feather with the 1st April beside it!

We didn't have a sewing teacher but Chappie bought us little traced doilies from the Glenreagh store. We did embroidery with the older girls teaching the younger ones and today there are a few samples of this beautiful work in Glenreagh's Memorial Museum. While the girls undertook sewing the boys did wood carving. The wooden boxes that the butter came in provided the boards for this kind of handiwork. Many fancy tea-pot stands and bread boards were made from these butter boxes.

After some years at school Chappie started to ride past us kids every Friday afternoon on his way up Lowanna way. We were soon to learn that there was a lady in his life. I am not sure where she lived but they later married. I know we had extra school holidays when our teacher, Chappie, broke his leg twice while playing football for Glenreagh and there was no replacement teacher for him, so the school was closed for an extended time.

There was only Earl Green and me in 6th Class when we both passed our QC Examination. From then we more or less helped the teacher out with the younger ones or learnt from some pink cards that were supplied by the Education

Department, or from a set of Encyclopaedias purchased by the P&C for our school.

My going to High School wasn't an option as it was the depression years. It was also a case of going away and boarding in Grafton. There was no regular or organised transport out of Tallawudjah Creek. It was a very isolated little community.

Pupils kind of filled in their time at school until they could leave at the mandatory age of 14, and then stay home and help in the home.

Many years later, when I was living at Llandilo, I had the good luck to meet up with two of my school mates, Andrew Symonds and Henry Green. We spent some enjoyable hours just reminiscing about our schooldays at Tallawudjah School. The question came up about Chappie and where did he go. We thought he may have gone to a school in the Kempsey area.

After their lovely visit to my Llandilo home in 1979, I was stirred to write this poem:

Bush Learning

The weather didn't matter
as we went our way each day.
Through the creek, along the road
we walked three mile each way.

The school was very tiny
but we didn't seem to care.
We played, we fought, we learned,
but best of all we shared.

The teacher was our hero
most times anyway,
When we didn't please him
we learnt to rue the day.

On nature walks he took us
to discover things on trees.
The moss, the leaves, the flowers,
and yes, the birds and bees.

When the day was stormy
and the creek height suddenly rose.
We knew we'd get home safely
as we hung on to his clothes.

In later years we've wondered
did he ever really fear.
That his horse and load would stumble
and lose the lives so dear?

Did he ever know it was Willie
that threw the cane down the loo.
Who pinned the tail on his coat
and made him an April Fool?

It took him a year to catch us
With his lyre bird under a box.
But catch us he did that morning
With the cunning of a fox.

There is one thing we know for certain
as we think of that little bush school.
Love and respect for the teacher
should be the golden rule.

We think of our school days often
as the lessons of life, we now learn.
The three R's were very important
but so was the love of our Ern.

copyright © Elizabeth Webb 1979

It was after this that I wanted to try to find my school teacher Chappie. At that time, I was into family history and was writing many letters trying to find knowledge. So I thought one more letter wouldn't matter.

I decided to write a Dear Editor letter to the local Kempsey newspaper, with the title, "Where are you Sir?"

Fortunately for me, Chappie answered and on one of our trips to the North Coast to see family, we called on him and his wife Kath. During our visit we learnt that although they were both having health problems they were looking forward to their upcoming Golden Wedding celebration. I took note of this date and was busily planning getting in touch with all his old Tallawudjah Creek students so we could just turn up and surprise him at the celebration. It didn't happen because they both became so unwell that the celebrations were cancelled, so floral tributes were sent to celebrate their special occasion.

Chappie wrote me a letter that was dated 17 March 1981 which is reproduced below:

Dear Bessie,

On this day 51 years ago I took up duties as Teacher-in-Charge of Tallawudjah Provisional School. On my Official Correspondence Forms, I had to enter the date of entry on Duty, so over a seven-year period I wrote 17/3/30 many times. I have very fond memories of those years.

Several times since my retirement I have had a dream that I have been re-appointed to Tallawudjah and I met all my old pupils outside the old school and began talking to them about their fathers and grandfathers. I never got further than into the porch before I woke up, sad that the dream had ended.

Very glad to receive your letter and thanks very much for the poem and it's quite good. I'm afraid I must have undermarked your literary efforts in the good old days. I don't think I was a very good teacher, I'd had two years training as Primary Assistant, and knew nothing about teaching in a small school or teaching infants. However, I must have picked it up as the years passed (judging by the results).

Chappie went on to thank me for the floral tributes that were sent and said when they recovered somewhat they were planning some kind of celebration for their Golden Wedding with their family in Sydney and he would let me know. Sadly, neither of them recovered good health. After I came to live in Glenreagh in 1982, their daughter visited us and we went back to the site of the school where her father taught.

I have always spoken to my growing family about my school days over the years, with fond memories and affection for Chappie, much to the surprise of my husband, Les, who had gone to school at Moss Vale and couldn't recall any of his teacher's names. In his primary school days, he had a different teacher each year.

The school weather shed was the scene of our Christmas break-ups. Another memory is the Annual Empire Day picnics, with all the kids-age races. The exciting event of chasing the Lolly Man was a highlight. Other school functions were held at our home. Across the creek from the school was Gray's barn and it was often the scene of school functions where locals had a lovely way of getting together and enjoying themselves.

Tallawudjah Creek school closed in 1944 and was removed to Lowanna where it is now part of Lowanna Primary School.

9. Connecting with the Outside

The first reference of Postal Services to this area was to the Postmaster General dated 6 September 1889. The Upper Orara Progress Association had called a meeting that was held at Coramba on 13 August 1889. Of the twenty-six signatories, twelve were residents of Tallawudjah and Glenreagh. They hoped for an extension of the South Grafton Kangaroo Creek Service. The route suggested was from Kangaroo Creek, via Back Creek, to McPherson's on Tallawudjah Creek, then through settlements up Tallawudjah Creek to Jones' settlement on little Nymboida, then via Nana Glen to meet the mailman at Coramba.

The Tallawudjah signatories were Thomas Keevers, William Simpson, Charles Simpson, John McBeath, Fred Garrett, James Gray, William Shipman, Richard Crabbe, T. McFarlane, John McPherson, and Reynolds.

As Glenreagh developed, requests were made and finally permission was given in July 1899 to appoint Mr Sweeney as

Postmaster of the first post office in Glenreagh. It was housed in the Glen Righ homestead.

I raised the question later in my adult life as to why there was only one phone up the Creek when I was young? I was informed, by Jack Shipman's family, that they were paid 30 pound per year to have it connected to their property for the use of the residents. I have no knowledge of what year this phone was installed. However, I do know it was there during my school years at Tallawudjah. The children in the Jack Shipman family said that when they heard a galloping horse coming along the road approaching their home, they knew it was an emergency of some kind and they would get ready to make a quick call.

10. Our Neighbours

I don't recall having any close neighbours prior to 1928 when we moved into our new home. We were now much closer to Johnsons who lived on the property adjoining ours. It was owned by the Dun brothers and the Johnson family lived in the home on the hill to the west of our new place. Bob Johnson went to school but I think only for a short period. The Duns resided in Glenreagh but owned a property up the creek.

Doug Hayes with his wife and family came to live in Granny's home after we vacated it in 1928. Mrs Hayes had very poor health as she had suffered a stroke and was chair bound. However, she still tried to care for her granddaughter, Mavis Moran, who was a little older than me. My mother would worry about this lonely little girl and used to send me over to play with her.

The Hayes household was made up of Mr Hayes, who was a teamster, and his son-in-law Tody Moran, who was my playmate Mavis' Dad. Mavis' mum had died some years earlier and she lived with her grandparents and their two sons Lachlan and Joe. Both sons worked in the timber industry.

All the menfolk of the household would go to work early and leave Mrs Hayes and Mavis on their own all day. Mavis had some kind of eye trouble and I recall her eye sort of half closed. I can only remember Mrs Hayes sitting in a cane armchair all day.

It was only when I returned to live in Glenreagh that I learnt more about the help that my Mum gave to the family.

Mavis Moran, 1936.

Mavis, now in her own home and assisting at functions in our community, after greeting me over a cuppa said, "You know Bessie, we would have starved only for your mother".

Mum would send me most days during the school holidays with something cooked, always in a container tied up in a tea-towel for easy carrying, to the Hayes home. I think Mum must have done it herself on school days, or my eldest sister Daphne may have, as she had left school by then. Mavis and I would help Mrs Hayes around the house on these days.

I can now remember my delight and happiness when I was little and Mrs Hayes bought me a lovely present of a little pair of garters to keep my socks up. They were something to see! I thought they were the prettiest things and showed them off to anyone who would look. Mavis and I had a good laugh about this when we re-connected.

Charles Simpson's property bounded Avery's Creek where Morning Star Creek crosses the roadway. From that crossing going south to the next creek crossing was the first section of some 160 acres owned by Reg Gill. This later became the property of my Uncle Jack Simpson, who married in 1927 and built a home on this property. This was the furthest home up Tallawudjah Creek.

I am unable to recall if there was any building on the Gill property when I was a child, but I do remember the Arold Shipman family home being burnt down. They moved to this location, and the reception after their daughter Jean's marriage, to Oliver Thornton in 1942, was held in a home there. I was their bridesmaid as Jean and I were friends from our days at Tallawudjah School.

Maggie Shipman and children

Arold and Maggie Shipman and their family were our nearest neighbours going towards Glenreagh and the Holder kids walked every school day with this Shipman family to school. The Shipman home was above the road and on the right side of the road on the rise of the hill. They had a tennis court on the flat area on the Glenreagh side of the present creek crossing.

Their children were Reg, Ivan, Harold, Jean and then later Bill. I think Reg had left school before I began and Bill hadn't started school. Jean was slightly older than me and she wasn't in my class at school.

11. Influence of the Railway

The last section of the railway line from Maitland to Grafton, which had commenced in Maitland in 1908, was not completed until 1922. It had reached Coffs Harbour by August 1915 and it had come from South Grafton to Glenreagh by September 1915. Due to financial struggles by the contractors plus the shortage of steel because of World War 1, and no doubt a shortage of workers, the last section of the rail line from Coffs to Glenreagh was not completed until 1922. The railway coming to Glenreagh appeared to open up the world to the folk living in this area.

The train service from Glenreagh to Grafton was a great help to the area as construction work on the Glenreagh to Dorrigo rail line was now underway, with this railway being opened on the 24 December 1924. It closed in 1972 due to heavy washaways of the rail line. Glenreagh, back then, was always spoken and written about as a town of great promise.

The train service from Glenreagh to South Grafton was a real help to Dad as he loved his pigs and could now see a way of getting them to the bacon factory. He set about to fatten one of the pigs for choice bacon for the winter months and we would have a ham leg for Christmas.

How were we to get the pig down to the Glenreagh Railway Station from Tallawudjah? Well, he had us kids to help. Early one morning we set off with food and drinks enough to last the day. I don't recall how many kids were in front but I think we took it in turns. Dad had a kid or two walking in front of the pigs. He took two at a time, with the other kids bringing up the rear. They all carried 'waddies' to wave at the pigs when necessary.

We slow walked them on what was known then as the Back Road. I can still take you to the mud hole where we stopped for the pigs to have a lay down and rest in the slushy waterhole while we ate our lunch.

I can't recall how we got over the traffic bridge. I think Dad had some work mates to help him, or timber men as us kids called them. I do remember Mum being there in the sulky to take us kids home so we didn't have to walk, and she had led a horse for Dad to ride home.

In due course Dad got his half side of the cured pig and it hung in its enclosed bag in the breeze way of our home. Our family enjoyed the freshly cut bacon whenever they wanted it.

Dad and Mum both came from hardy backgrounds and knew the importance of keeping us well fed.

One year when I was about 9 years old he decided to take we three younger children to the Dorrigo Show. This meant an early rise, with Dad on one horse and we three on our pony as we rode through our property to Timber Top to catch the train. When the horses were attended to, Dad told us where to stand as Timber Top did not have a platform as it was only a siding. He was going to stand on the line and stop the train, and that is what he did! He just put his hand up and the train stopped. We thought he was wonderful.

We had a great day at the show, fairy floss and all the other goodies. It was nearing nightfall when we returned to get on our horses for the ride home. Dad put my youngest sister in the middle of us and fastened his belt around us in case she went to sleep and fell off. He then talked to us all the way home. In later years, when we spoke about that day, he told us that he had arranged with the engine driver about stopping the train with him helping Dad to get us up and in the train.

When I was doing research for my history book about Glenreagh I found some interesting snippets.

One of the early newspapers wrote that the train had transported a coffin into South Grafton for burial. The train was met at the Station by the Undertaker's van and the funeral service was held then.

I also read a report that when they were building the Glenreagh to Dorrigo railway line, there were 300 'navvies' standing on the Glenreagh Railway station ready to board the train to go home for their Christmas holiday. The railway workers of that era were called 'navvies' after the machine that laid the line was called a navigator.

Another newspaper report of the day about the railway line to Dorrigo.

The Mussared family from Nana Glen milked their herd of cows at their farm in the morning. They then loaded all their farm gear, cattle and furniture on the train and got everything to their new Dorrigo property in time to do the afternoon milking.

Besides all manner of freight that the train took, from pigs into the bacon factory at South Grafton, some farmers had no other way of sending their cream to the butter factory than by train.

The train service in the early days meant so much more than just moving people around.

12. Characters of the Bush

During the depression years there were many people, swaggies or tramps, walking the roads looking for work. I do not recall seeing any up Tallawudjah Creek but when I was living at Granny's farm and going to school in Glenreagh, I witnessed many swagmen walking the road, or camping under a tree. It was not until later in my life that I learned why they always called at my Grandma's farm to do a job, such as cutting fire wood before getting a meal. They sometimes did gardening. She was very generous to these men and sometimes I used to think she knew them from somewhere. It was really a sign of the times with everyone struggling during this period but us kids did not know about this until years later. As kids we were never without nourishing food, loving parents and a bed to sleep in at night.

There were quite a few individual characters living in and around the area. I remember there was a lone Indian man camped near the creek crossing at Arold Shipman's property when I walked to school. He used to give us Johnny Cakes most mornings on our way past his tent, which was at the side of the roadway. I can't recall him speaking to us, just smiling and waving at us kids on our way to school. I have wondered now, where did he work or was he was just searching for his fortune.

Bob Morris is another character to come to mind. Bob lived alone somewhere in the bush towards Timber Top and often entertained himself by playing musical instruments. He had a nice looking pony and sulky which he used to drive around and visit people. I think he went through Dad's property to get to his camp at times.

At one time, Bob, with his pony and sulky, took up a small haberdashery business. He had two large suitcases full of sewing needs such as cotton, needles, children's socks, and adult's underwear. He used to call on the homes from time to time with these items.

He would call at our place quite a lot. I was only a schoolchild in those days and Bob would play with us, no matter what the game was, whether rounders, chasings or hide and seek.

I recall that we had a cattle dog named Bruce and he was always with us kids wherever we were. If Bob happened to catch one of us while playing, Bruce would immediately grab Bob's trousers in his teeth and hang on until he was ordered to let go by us kids.

Bruce was a great dog, loved by all our family and he was always around us kids. He did grow to an old age and one day we came out of school, ready for the long walk home and Bruce had died while he was waiting for us. An old dog faithful to the end.

Mr and Mrs Doug Hayes and their family were living on Granny's place at this time with their sons Lachie and Joe Hayes. Tody Moran and his daughter Mavis were also living there. Mrs Hayes was confined to a chair and there was a lady who came to care for her that Bob quite admired.

I remember one hot summer day when the road gang that was building the new road, which eventually was to divide my Dad's farm, had ceased their work for the day and were camped near our swimming hole. They always had a dip in the creek after they knocked off work, and Dad said we could watch them. They liked diving off the large rock that bounded the deep waterhole. Bob often came down to swim with them.

Mr & Mrs Hayes in their sulky.

This day we were high up on the bank that overlooked the swimming scene below us when Bob came up out of the water to climb up on the rock. Instead of wearing swimming attire, he was dressed in a pair of ladies Milanese undies that were very wet and one might say revealing. My dad had just ridden his horse home from the bush and saw his kids laughing and no doubt hearing the workers making similar noises, he also came to look. He laughed about it afterwards, but he made sure his kids beat a hasty retreat back to their home. From then on the viewing area was declared a no go zone for us kids.

Dad was a non-swimmer but he wanted all his kids to learn and he sought out two of the workmen to teach us at weekends. They also played tennis with us kids on the tennis court that he built for us. Mum played tennis but as Dad couldn't, he learnt at the same time as his kids.

In thinking about the folk who lived up the creek during my childhood many of them could play some kind of instrument, mainly the old button accordion. Arold Shipman used to play all kinds of tunes on the gum leaf. Almost every home had a piano or pianola. Folk entertained themselves and young kids were encouraged to sing at the house or barn parties.

I can recall another character, Luke Simmons, singing at the Christmas tree nights at Tallawudjah Creek school and other party type functions. He wasn't a good singer. There was always food served and Luke would tease all the mothers about their cooking. He was fussy about what cakes or pastry he ate beforehand as he didn't want the food to ruin his voice. I also remember one musical program taking part in the school's weather shed near the tennis court, with one of the father's throwing a broom up on the roof to try and stop Luke singing, then rushing around to the front pretending it was the kids who threw the broom.

Tallawudjah Creek and Glenreagh were part of the same area as far as characters were concerned. Jim Maxwell, known as Starlight, was a returned man from World War 1 and he roamed all over the area and at Back Creek. Jim had a long-based, over 7 feet (2 metres), wheelbarrow, and his occupation was doing cartage jobs for people. I recall seeing bricks and other farming type needs on his wheelbarrow but Jim also had a drinking problem. Dad, also a returned man, had a soft spot for Jim and would always offer him a cup of tea or a meal whenever he was anywhere near our home.

Jim called at our place one night when Dad was home minding his three younger daughters while Mum had ridden to Glenreagh with the two older children to a social outing. Dad at that time was adding the kitchen to the existing home and the added verandah boards were being cut ready for nailing the next day or two. Jim came up the steps and walked on the loose floorboards and they gave way and he went down underneath the flooring. As there was a noise, Dad went out to investigate, only to find Jim down between the flooring joists. Dad had been in the kitchen playing cards with us younger kids.

Dad was a fairly big man, and he got down under the flooring trying to get Jim up, who was affected by drink. It proved to be a considerable task with the loose boards and a confined space. Of course, us kids rushed out to see what the commotion was about. By this time they were both cursing, and we were soon told to get back inside by the fire and shut the kitchen door. At some time later, sanity must have rained on them both, as they had a cuppa and a laugh before Jim went on his way.

Dad always spoke fondly of Jim and often quoted him to us kids about not rushing at things but 'to think things out' like Jim did and so should we.

Jim had to move a 1000-gallon tank on his wheelbarrow from Glenreagh down into Back Creek area. I know it was in the early 1930's and if you travel from Glenreagh up the Tallawudjah Creek road you will see a fairly big hill east in front of you. I am not sure if it has a name. In the early days the mail used to come over this hill from Coutts Crossing by horseback to McPherson's receiving Post office delivery place at Tallawudjah.

When Jim got to the top of this hill with his wheelbarrow, he thought that going downhill the other side his load might get away from him. So he took it off the wheelbarrow and wheeled it down empty with the tank bobbling on his back at every step as he walked before it.

When he got to a flatter area the tank was put back on the wheelbarrow.

Tallawudjah Creek... and Me

All the kids in the area of the creek and Glenreagh grew up on a diet of George Shipman's yarns. George, a bachelor, lived and owned land on the back road to Glenreagh.

George used to love his daily rides on his horse to the hotel and he used to play cards with anyone he could find. He would leave his horse on the unfenced spare block opposite the hotel. George would have a few drinks, and if he was a little late in leaving the hotel, the horse would come across the road and put its head in the bar door, much to the amusement of the drinkers. It was always close to the 6 o'clock closing time for hotels at that time when the horse would undertake its daily responsibility to look after George.

George loved to tell stories of his fishing experience in the Orara river at Glenreagh.

He told us that he once hooked a big cod and it kept breaking his line. So he decided to go fishing with a fishing hook fastened to a trace chain. Feeling tired this afternoon he fastened the chain to his leg while he went to sleep. When he woke up he was miles down the river and the chain had broken as the fish was that big. George used to tell folk if they went down by the river and sat quietly looking at the water, they might hear a slight jangly sound as the big cod would swim up and down, dangling the chain on the riverbed stones.

When World War 1 broke out in 1914 there was a recruiting drive that came through Glenreagh with many local men enlisting. One of them was Claude Darwin who was a single man working in the area on the railway. He had migrated from England some time earlier and when he enlisted, he said he would bring home a yarn from the war that would top some of George's tall stories.

I was in our schoolroom doing some dusting for our teacher, Chappie, at Tallawudjah Creek School when we heard this story from my brother Charlie through the open window, repeating the yarn that Claude brought back from World War 1 for George. I always remember how Chappie laughed.

He also had been at the end of many of George's jokes or tall stories, as we kids called them, and no, Charlie did not get into any trouble from Chappie for swearing.

Here is Claude's yarn:

Would you believe that over there in England there were quite a few aeroplanes being built with lots of young Australian pilots learning to fly them. However, there were lots of accidents and many were killed.

Would you believe that they invented spring-heeled wellington boots so that the pilots could bounce up and down when the plane crashed. As a matter of fact, one pilot bounced up and down for two weeks while we were over there, and they had to shoot him to stop him!

George's reply was, "If you told half the buggers around here, they just would not believe it!"

Some more of George's yarns:

George was going to Grafton in his horse and sulky to get some greyhound pups. On his way home he could see a bad storm coming up so he hit the horse to make it go faster. On arriving at Glenreagh, he did not have a drop of rain on him but when he looked in the kerosene drum, where he had the pups, they were all drowned.

George was growing pumpkins at his place on what is now known as Shipmans Road, and he rode in one day to Granny Shipman's home in the village. He told her, "I do not know what to do with my pumpkins. They are growing so fast that the bottoms of them are getting worn through as the vines are pulling them along."

George rode his bike on the way to Grafton and as he went down the hill at the Bluff Bridge, he came off the bike and landed up in a tree. George was taken to hospital and when he came out, two weeks later, the wheels of the bike were still spinning up in the tree.

George took his slide and horse down to the creek to collect some water in drums. When he arrived back at his house the slide was still at the creek. The green hide traces had become wet as he filled the drums and had stretched. George decided to leave the horse attached to the slide and was surprised to find, as the greenhide traces dried, that the slide arrived at his home by itself.

13. Reflections

As this book draws to a close, my thoughts are again on the creek of my youth.

What part in my development, as I left my childhood scene and moved into the more formative years of adulthood, did living there play out in later life. Recently, in my 101st year, I was part of a discussion about differences between country and city reared children. The main difference we all thought is that country reared folk are generally ever ready to share and to help one another.

This discussion left me with thoughts of 'the Creek' and my beginnings. Although somewhat initially isolated I have witnessed so many of the world's new things. From craning our small necks out of the school windows at Tallawudjah to try and catch sight of Smithy's plane flying high in the sky as he raced those days from England.

The first time we had electricity in our home was when I was 18.

I also was witness to the anxious concern of my father. He was a retired World War I veteran and took on the duties of a warden during World War II. Also the hard work that women did as the men left for the war. I was a hard working teenager during the Second World War. We had many farewells for our soldier friends, some becoming our penfriends, as they went to serve their country.

We still tried to play sport, attend social functions and share a meal with neighbours. I even found the love of my life during this trying time. After marrying in Grafton in December 1944, I left the north coast for the south coast of NSW, a few months before the war was over.

Another first was getting a TV, then later watching the first man walk on the moon. As computers and all kinds of electronics take over, it's a challenge for the older generation to adapt their thinking, but adapt we must.

What was there about this small isolated place where just a few families lived, worked and had such fun as small communities did back then. "You need your neighbour" as my Dad would say, as he shared his wisdom and love with us kids. I sat next to Dad at our meal table all my single life and would often sneak a drink from his cup of tea. My memory of my Mum's tenacity is remembered by her positive encouragement of the youngest child that their little billy of water was life-giving to our homegrown vegies and plants.

Over the years since my childhood 'the Creek' has gone back to the bush as old time residents have passed away and life changes have taken place. A recent trip up the creek shows a few new homes are being constructed and a general re-settling is taking place.

When I was six years old and I went with Mum in the horse and sulky to Glenreagh by the long road, we drove through Tallawudjah Creek eight times to get to the shop and post office. Today we cross only one bridge and the tyres of the car do not get wet.

I have been blessed that Tallawudjah Creek provided the foundation for my fortunate life.

Reflections

Travelling through the country, every now and then you'll see
where a home once stood, near a leaning bough of a gnarled old apple tree.
Struggling little flowers brightly bloom through spindly grass,
and perfumed honeysuckle soothes the senses as you pass.

Old slab walls on the rusting barn all have a dangerous lean
while the garden, once so full of pride, is a dismal unloved scene.
Giant pear trees stand in grandeur in an orchard corner bare,
the fruit unpicked and rotting….. there's no one there to care.

Rusty broken relics that lay half hidden in the soil,
Speak of shattered dreams encountered and days of long hard toil.
And cattle, softly lowing, in the distance o'er the hill
Makes you ponder, "If the rain had come would the family be here still?"

Tallawudjah Creek... and Me

Was the struggle for survival lost through
sickness, drought or fire,
or were they called to 'come on home' from
someone who is higher.
Did another generation seek a different
style of life
settling in a busy city....
far from the country strife?

Many fleeting visions of times that
might have been
stirs family recollections,
as you survey and dream.
The hills hold all the secrets of the struggles
and the test
then you leave as twilight deepens,
praying "Dear Lord, may they rest".

copyright © Elizabeth Webb 1987

Previous books by Elizabeth Webb:

Glenreagh 1858-1983	1983
William and Sarah Keevers	1989
Crows Can't Count	1994
Glenreagh, A Town of Promise	1998
Grandma's Garland	2001
Glenreagh The Railway Heritage (Chapter 6)	2004
Christ Church Glenreagh 1914-2014	2014
Aren't We Glad He is Ours	2002

www.ingramcontent.com/pod-product-compliance
Lightning Source LLC
Chambersburg PA
CBHW062044290426
44109CB00026B/2730